Desert Spirit Places

Desert Spirit Places

The Sacred Southwest

Brad Karelius

Foreword by Ron Dart

RESOURCE *Publications* · Eugene, Oregon

DESERT SPIRIT PLACES
The Sacred Southwest

Copyright © 2018 Brad Karelius. All rights reserved. Except for brief quotations in critical publications or reviews, no part of this book may be reproduced in any manner without prior written permission from the publisher. Write: Permissions, Wipf and Stock Publishers, 199 W. 8th Ave., Suite 3, Eugene, OR 97401.

Resource Publications
An Imprint of Wipf and Stock Publishers
199 W. 8th Ave., Suite 3
Eugene, OR 97401

www.wipfandstock.com

PAPERBACK ISBN: 978-1-5326-5465-7
HARDCOVER ISBN: 978-1-5326-5466-4
EBOOK ISBN: 978-1-5326-5467-1

Manufactured in the U.S.A.   02/20/19

This book is written with gratitude
for Don Mose and Harry Nez,
spiritual guides in the Dinétah.
May we walk in Beauty.

> ... for most the desert is not a place but an experience that takes hold of you, becomes part of you, turns you inside out, opens the City to contemplation, to a long, loving look at the real.
>
> WALTER J. BURGHARDT, SJ, *CONTEMPLATION: A LONG, LOVING LOOK AT THE REAL*

Contents

Permissions | xiii
Acknowledgments | xv
Foreword by Ron Dart | xvii

1. Cedar Mesa, Utah—By Way of Introduction | 3
2. Grand Canyon, Arizona—Living on Bread and Water | 9
3. From Lone Pine, California, to the Valley of the Kings
   —The Curse of the Dust Devils | 17
4. El Sanctuario de Chimayo, New Mexico—Holy Healing | 22
5. Zuni Pueblo, New Mexico—Zuni Fetish: Living Stones | 32
6. Abiquiu, New Mexico—Passionate Christians | 40
7. Orange Park Acres, Southern California—Leaving the House of Prayer | 52
8. Three Mesas: Hopi, Arizona—Sacred Masks | 59
9. Santa Ana and Olancha Creek, California
   —Insane for the Light: Psychosis and Mysticism | 65
10. Mystery Valley, Navajo Nation—The Huge Hogan | 74
11. Poverty Hills, California—Digging for Treasure | 82
12. Sunset Crater, Arizona—Eyes to See | 87
13. North of Santa Fe, New Mexico—The Penitentes | 93
14. Monument Valley, Utah—Eclipse of the Moon | 101
15. Navajo Nation, Four Corners—Earth Medicine | 105
16. Mesa Verde, Colorado—The Kiva as Sacred Ground | 113

17. Antelope Valley, California—Seeing the Divine Within | 119
18. The Dinétah, Arizona-New Mexico—Tony Hillerman: Reading the Signs | 126
19. Alabama Hills, California—Desert Night Sky | 134
20. Where We Are Now—Second Naiveté | 142

Bibliography | 149
Index | 157

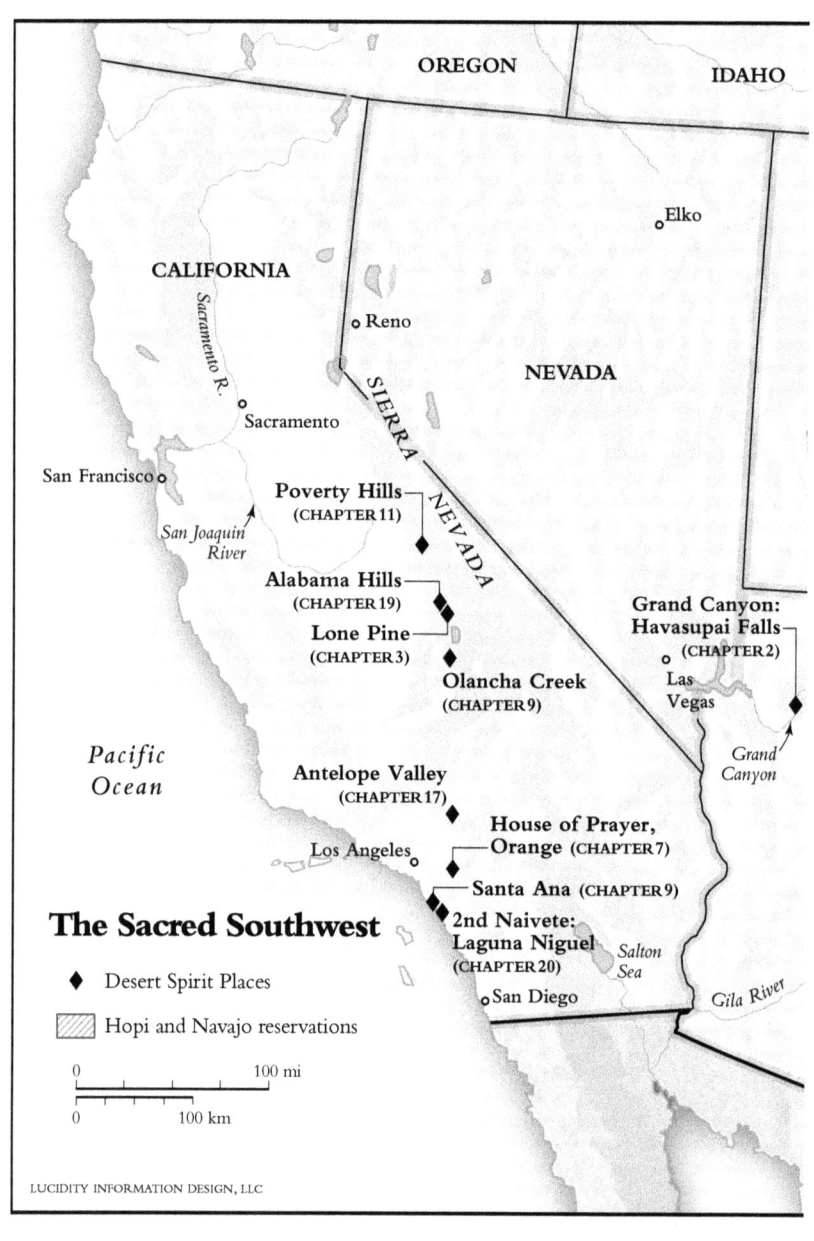

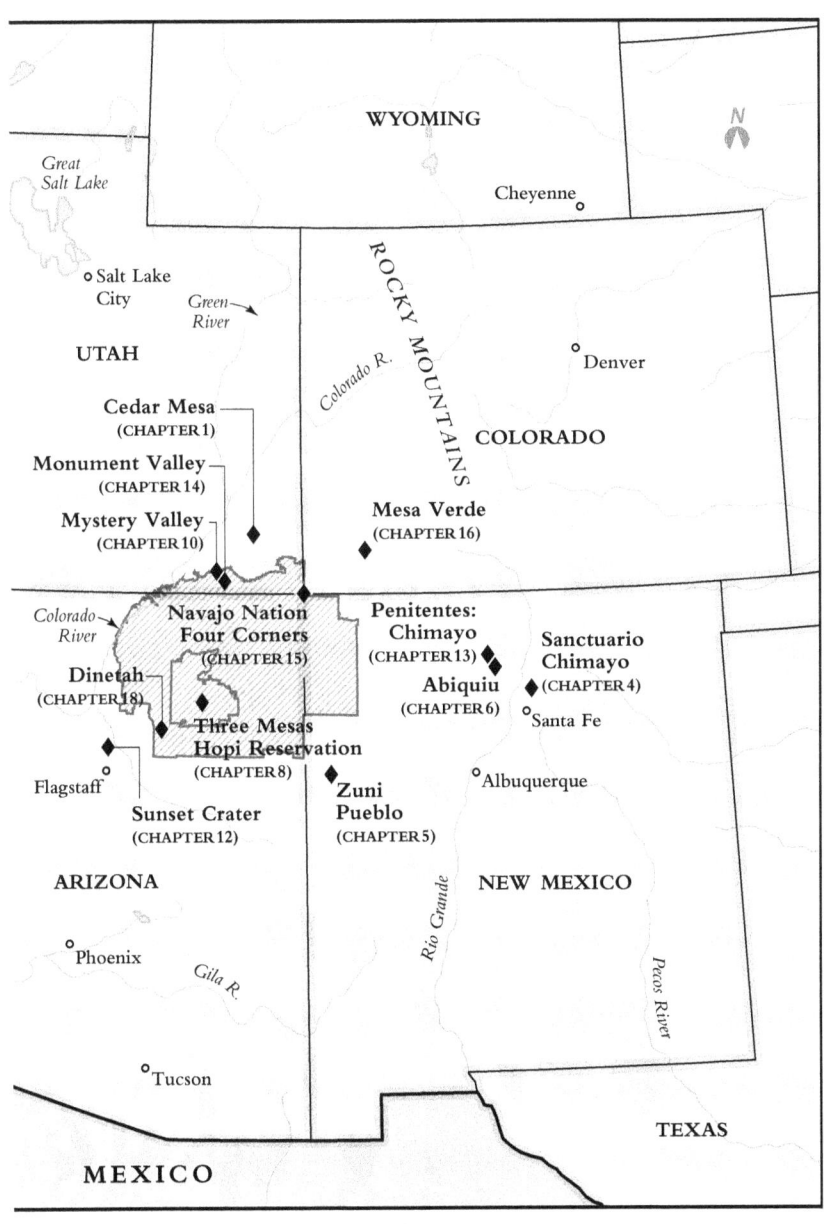

Permissions

EVERY EFFORT HAS BEEN made to trace the holders of copyrighted material used in this book. The author is grateful for permission to quote from the following:

The Wisdom of the Desert by Thomas Merton, copyright © 1960 by The Abbey of Gethsemani, Inc. Reprinted by permission of New Directions Publishing Corp.

Quotation from p. 77 from *Dance Hall of the Dead* by Tony Hillerman. Copyright © 1973 by Anthony G. Hillerman. Reprinted by permission of HarperCollins Publishers.

Two excerpts from pp. 33–34 from *Pilgrim at Tinker Creek* by Annie Dillard. Copyright © 1974 by Annie Dillard. Reprinted by permission of HarperCollins Publishers.

Excerpt from pp. 56–57 from *Silent Music* by William Johnston. Copyright © 1974 by Brian Finegan, trustee under William Johnston Trust Agreement No. 1. Reprinted by permission of HarperCollins Publishers.

Thank you to Don Mose for permission to quote him in an interview at Mystery Valley, Utah, October 2017.

Thank you to Curtis Brown, Ltd. for permission in the United Kingdom and British Commonwealth excluding Canada to quote from *Dance Hall of the Dead* by Tony Hillerman. Copyright © 1973 by Tony Hillerman. Reprinted by permission of Curtis Brown, Ltd. All rights reserved.

Excerpt from pp. 221–22 from *The Solace of Fierce Landscapes* by Belden Lane. Copyright © 1998 by Belden Lane. Reprinted by permission of Oxford University Press USA.

PERMISSIONS

The Spiritual Life of Children by Robert Coles. Copyright © 1990 by Robert Coles. Reprinted by permission of Houghton Mifflin Harcourt. All rights reserved.

Earth Is My Mother, Sky Is My Father by Trudy Griffen-Pierce. Copyright © 1992 by Trudy Griffen-Pierce. Reprinted by permission of University of New Mexico Press.

Zuni Fetishes and Carvings by Kent McManis. Copyright © 2004 by Kent McManis. Reprinted by permission of Rio Nuevo Publishers.

"Psychiatric Drugs and Healing" by P. J. Johnston, *America Magazine*, April 22, 2014. Reprinted by permission of *America Magazine*.

Believing in Place: A Spiritual Geography of the Great Basin by Richard V. Francaviglia. Copyright © 2003 by Richard V. Francaviglia. Reprinted by permission of University of Nevada Press.

Acknowledgments

THANK YOU TO THOSE who read the manuscript and offered important criticism and ideas: Dr. Walter Brueggemann of Columbia Theological Seminary; Dr. John R. Stilgoe of Harvard University; Dr. Richard V. Francaviglia of the University of Texas and Center for Greater Southwestern Studies; Dr. Beverly G. Six of Sul Ross State University; Anne Hillerman of Santa Fe, New Mexico; Dr. Ronald Dart, University of Fraser Valley, British Columbia; Dr. David Jasper of the University of Glasgow, Scotland; Professor Philip Sheldrake of Cambridge University; Dr. Ronald James of the Nevada State Historic Preservation Office; Dr. Belden Lane of St. Louis University; Alex Ross of *The New Yorker* magazine; and Dr. Kerry Walters of Gettysburg College.

I am grateful for my spiritual director, Fr. Gordon Moreland, SJ, of the Roman Catholic Diocese of Orange, California. His prayerful encouragement has guided me through many interior deserts over the past twenty years.

Thank you to Robert Cronan of Lucidity Information Design, LLC for creating the map with chapter locations.

Thank you to my philosophy students at Saddleback Community College, Mission Viejo, California, for what you have shared with me in your spiritual journeys. I am grateful for my dean, Dr. Kevin O'Connor, and for my department chair, Dr. Basil Smith, for the privilege of being an instructor on the subject of the world's religions.

Finally, thank you to Denis Clarke and Source Books. Denis has been the patient copy editor of this book and lovingly polished the rough work. Over the years, we have shared the Micah's Way ministry with the poor and homeless in Santa Ana and I am blessed to have his participation in this project.

Foreword

> In my beginning is my end
> In my end is my beginning
> —T.S. Eliot, *East Coker*

IT IS WITH MUCH fondness that I remember reading Derwas Chitty's *The Desert a City* (1966) and Sister Benedicta Ward's *The Desert Christian: The Sayings of the Desert Fathers* (1975) in the late 1970s, for an MA thesis on John Cassian. Many of the more contemplative Christians from the second to the sixth centuries CE knew the desert was the place in which a deeper transformation and self-understanding could be birthed. I had also found T. S. Eliot's *The Wasteland* and *Four Quartets* compact poetic missives on seeing into the core of the multiple distractions of the modern world and the path to the contemplative vision, of much assistance on my journey. Thomas Merton had been taken by the literal and metaphorical notion of the "desert" in three of his finest books at various stages of his life: *Bread in the Wilderness*, *The Wisdom of the Desert*, and *Woods, Shore, Desert*.

The Biblical motif of the "desert" as embodied in the Jewish exodus to freedom and Jesus' three temptations cannot be missed—the tensions between freedom and bondage, addiction and liberty cannot be ignored in the desert metaphor. The notion of the desert as a place in the soul and society in which diverse diversions are seen for what they truly are (Eliot's insights on being "distracted from distraction by distraction") speak much about the fantasy of many of the addictive tendencies of the capitalist West, the courage to let go of them (no distractions in the desert), and the being open and receptive to a deeper reality of being.

Foreword

Even C. S. Lewis's *The Horse and His Boy* features the desert and the role of the hermit in bringing wisdom to a situation thick with conflict. But such a wisdom and contemplative way of seeing and being is countercultural in our frenetic and driven Western culture and ethos—we are, in short, addicted to and slaves of a hyperactivism or, to use the classical notion, the *vita activa*—the task of detoxifying is not an easy one, but Father Brad Karelius does point to such possibilities, the desert metaphor, his guiding light and Polaris North Star.

It was, then, with much delight that I read and inwardly digested Father Brad Karelius's *The Spirit in the Desert: Pilgrimages to Sacred Sites in the Owens Valley* (2009) and *Encounters with the World's Religions: The Numinous on Highway 395* (2015). The journey of the soul to the empty places in which the real ascesis is about facing into many of the sadnesses, disappointments, and tragedies of life and seeing them as means of a deeper Divine Love cannot be missed. Yes, there is, of course, the literal desert as a place of seeming barrenness, devoid of life, but those who have dwelt in the desert (my wife and I have done so many times) for long know it intimately as a place of abundant life, flowering, and beauty—much hinges on the seeing eye and receptive mind and imagination. Father Karelius has, yet again, opened up deeper and fuller vistas of insight in this his newest book, *Desert Spirit Places: The Sacred Southwest*. Needless to say, the literal places in various sites in the Southwest of the United States (Utah, Arizona, New Mexico, California) are, to use the Celtic notion, "thin places," in which, when the eyes of the souls are properly rinsed, an inner center is lived—in which suffering is seen from a different perspective.

Father Karelius, rightly so, is less concerned with a vast array of spiritual forms, techniques, and disciplines that are, in principle, meant to starve the "false self" or Old Adam/Eve—he is much more concerned about the inner receptivity that can awaken one and all to a thinness of the soul and the birth of our new being—such a pathway unites us with God and with one another. This means the desert, in the deepest sense, is more about dying to what needs to be released so that the bird of our new being can break through its constrictive and life-denying shell and, in time, take wings and fly. Such a journey, though, has taken Father Karelius, as a husband, father, priest, and college lecturer, in directions he never would have anticipated when younger. Such a desert was about letting go, letting go many times so that a deeper, more real and more mature life could be lived within the

Foreword

context of his parish, family, friendships, and teaching life. *Desert Spirit Places* can be read at many levels.

There are, of course, the desert places to visit, but if a tourist-style visit is all that is done, the deeper wisdom will be missed. There is, further down the trail, the way the desert can massage and reshape the lines, tendons, tissues, and tendencies of the soul and body—much hinges on how far the honest and eager pilgrim wishes to go—play it safe or go to the places of death and rebirth; the former is the way of the spiritual dilettante and voyeur, the latter the way of the deified and transformed saint who enters the strains and struggles of world with the wing of contemplation and insight on one side and on the other, the wing of passion for justice and mercy.

The sheer beauty of *Desert Spirit Places* is the way Father Karelius threads together, in a vulnerable and transparent way, on a finely textured tapestry, his life journey with those he has met—there is something quite earthy and honest about such a book. Father Karelius has for forty-five years been both a priest and college professor at Messiah Episcopal Church in Santa Ana and Saddleback Community College, Mission Viejo, California. This is but the beginning, though.

Many who attended Father Karelius's parish were rooted and grounded in both indigenous backgrounds and immigrant culture. This means a softness and tenderness to such life journeys had to be heeded. It was, though, by the soul being turned to such historic ways of life that the "buffered self" of the rationalistic, "scientific," and empirical wing of the Enlightenment is eased and becomes more porous. The fact that Father Karelius has a son who is disabled also deepens the journey, and many of the chapters in *Desert Spirit Places* describe visits Father Karelius made with his wife (Jan) and son (Erik) to such sacred and thin places. The task of weakening the "buffered self" (so well dissected by Charles Taylor) is at the heart and core of *Desert Spirit Places* as each short, illuminating chapter walks the reader into revealing experiences of gentle yet real moments of insight.

The telling reality of Father Karelius's high-grade prostate cancer cannot be missed in this tale of a spiritual quest. I found myself, often, joining Father Karelius, his wife, son, and daughter (Katie) on many of their trips to such sacred sites. The layered nature of varied and various First Nations spirituality are existentially told in a most inviting and instructive way. The reality of such ongoing encounters makes for life-changing moments. In short, this is not just a book about the metaphor of the desert; it is much more about desert dwellers and the time-tried wisdom they still have to

FOREWORD

offer to those with eyes to see and ears to hear. The "buffered self" has indeed much letting go to do if the "Real Self" is ever to crack through the constricting shell and take to the blue canopy above.

Desert Spirit Places is, in many ways, about reclaiming and recovering an older and deeper way of being in which time and eternity, spirit and matter meet and greet, are one, and go dancing together. The severing of such an integrated historic connection is what Father Karelius sees as the illness of our age, and the return to such an older way inevitably reveals what has been lost by becoming modern, yet also what has been gained by becoming modern. Holy sites do not always bring healing in a superstitious or snake-oil sort of way and modern medicine can often deal with illnesses that sacred places do not—such is the dilemma of living with the past and present as we trek into the future; the subtle yet surgical way that Father Karelius ponders and lives into such complex realities cannot be missed in this autobiographical yet perennially significant book. Chapter by chapter we are taken on a journey into ways and means of heeding desert spirit places in the sacred Southwest, but sorting and sifting their speech is ever the dilemma. The fact that Father Karelius is a priest means he returns, again and again, to the sacramental theology that so informs and infuses his contemplative vision. But, such a sacramental theology is informed by visits and lessons learned at such spirit places.

I mentioned at the beginning of this introduction how the superb research of Derwas Chitty and Sister Benedicta Ward had done much to bring to the fore the motif of desert spirituality in the early centuries of the Church's life. Both Chitty and Ward focused on the desert as place and metaphor in Lower Egypt, Upper Egypt, Nitria and Scetis, Syria, Asia Minor, and Palestine. The genius of *Desert Spirit Places* is the way Father Karelius has illuminated for the attentive reader the way the notion of the desert is a perennial theme in the contemplative journey and, equally important, the way the desert drama and tale has unfolded in the Southwest of the USA.

There is no need, in short, to excessively focus on the wisdom of the early abbas and ammas of the deserts in the Middle East—the American Southwest has its own unique tale to tell for those who are willing to shake off the skin of their self-encapsulated and buffered ego and see what is yet to be more fully seen. Indeed, as Eliot noted in "East Coker," our end is but our beginning and our new beginning points towards a more sacred end. Father Karelius has done yeoman work for us in *Desert Spirit Places*

Foreword

in living and pointing to the markings of such better endings and fuller beginnings.

Do purchase and inwardly digest this pure-gold beauty of a book—the steps taken, paths walked,m and sights seen will both root the soul and give wings to it at the same time (and, as a special boon, an apt and poignant history of the American Southwest will be the added gift).

Ron Dart
University of Fraser Valley
Abbotsford, BC
2018

Cedar Mesa Moon House Ruin, Utah. 2012. U.S. Bureau of Land Management.

1.

Cedar Mesa, Utah
—By Way of Introduction . . .

> The further you go into the desert, the closer you come to God.
> —ancient arabic proverb[1]

LOOSE ROCKS TUMBLE INTO the ravine hundreds of feet below as I walk with our son, Erik, beside me. He is disabled. I hold firmly onto his left arm, making sure that he keeps to the inside of the winding path carved into the massive granite shelf. Janice, my wife, is following with the ever-vigilant service dog, Ms. Ella, a standard poodle.

Early afternoon sun beats upon our Stetson straw hats, but a cooling breeze caresses us, coming up from Monument Valley. We are hiking into Cedar Mesa, an ancient plateau west of Blanding, Utah. The numerous canyons of these parts were inhabited by the Clovis people, going back thirteen thousand years. The extensive ruins of Clovis culture—many of which have not been seen by non-Native Americans—attract hikers to this remote part of the world, and right now we are heading to one of the more accessible public sites.

I continue to fix my attention on Erik. His sturdy, muscled thighs and calves testify to the miles he walks each day back home with his caregiver, Bill Remington. We have almost forgotten Erik's feeble, skeletal appearance of a dozen years ago: wheelchair-bound, surviving on intravenous nutrition. He had been struck down with encephalitis when he was four, which left him with a severely scarred brain and the mind of an eternal

---

1. Quoted in Lane, *Solace of Fierce Landscapes*, 150.

four-year-old. He still has seizures every day. But now, at thirty, he is taller than me, almost six feet, with broad shoulders and chest. The early scans indicated to the neurologist that the motor area of the brain was so damaged that Erik would not be able to walk again; yet here he is, walking beside me, step by step into Wonderland.

Erik's gaze is far away—perhaps an absence seizure. We say that at such moments he is "on one bar." But that will change in a few minutes and he will begin to rattle on with us as we walk.

Speaking of receptivity, given our fixation with iPhones and our shortening attention spans, the good news is that there are no "bars" here. There is the sun, there are thunderclouds moving in from the west, the brown-tailed hawk circling above, the rabbit rustling in the juniper bush, hiding from Ms. Ella. But the frantic, hyperconnected outside world does not obtrude here. The trail in the granite slab twists around blind corners.

And I am thinking that the trail is like the past twenty-five years with Erik, twisting around blind corners. You never know what will happen next: he can bounce up one morning singing all the lyrics from a 1950s rock-'n'-roll song and in the afternoon he is languishing in the intensive care unit.

Erik will act as guide to some of the places we visit in this book. He will share his experience in his own way. And I will be the guide for other places, the desert retreats where I have found the solace and strength to support our family on an uncertain trail.

So, I had better lay out something of my résumé—you don't want a guide you know nothing about.

For forty-five years I have had the dual vocation of parish priest and college professor. Thirty of those years were spent as pastor of Messiah Episcopal Church in Santa Ana, California. I am retired now. The historic church building is located in the Logan Barrio, an area crowded with five-storey apartment buildings, where it is not a surprise to find three families sharing one apartment. Though there have been improvements, grinding poverty and resurgent gang violence continue to gnaw at the lives of everyone, especially the children and teens.

During my first years in Santa Ana I was taught to read, write and speak Spanish by a charismatic Cubana, Raquel Salcinez. This opened the door to my celebrating Mass in Spanish and to working with Father Christopher Smith of St. Joseph's Roman Catholic Church, and with the Sisters of St. Joseph of Orange, to create a number of programs that would counter the evil forces haunting our neighborhood. We started Hands Together—A

Cedar Mesa, Utah—By Way of Introduction

Center for Children; three early-childhood centers, including one for homeless children; the St. Joseph Ballet for young Latinas; Taller San Jose (St. Joseph's Workshop) to give solid work training for older boys and girls who were breaking away from the gangs; the Noah Project, which provided after-school tutoring and club activities for junior and senior high-schoolers; and we helped the local Catholic Worker ministry, and a hospice for impoverished people with AIDS.

The Spanish language brought me into the lives of my Latino parishioners, many of whom were undocumented. We celebrated the sacraments, quinceañeras, Primera Communion, and powerful public processions through the streets of the barrio and downtown on Good Friday night, Palm Sunday and on the Feast of Our Lady of Guadalupe. In the midst of desperate lives, the sacred permeated daily life—which contrasted greatly with the compartmentalized spirituality of many of my Anglo parishioners.

I became immersed in the spiritual traditions of the indigenous Americans and immigrants of the barrio. I ministered to the sick alongside Mexican curanderos (healers) and Cuban Santeria priests. Parish life was complemented by animistic, pre-Columbian traditions from Latin America. The Church of the Messiah became a center of extraordinary diversity. For example, David Vazquez, who was soon to become a parish leader, was the son of the chief of a remote village near Puebla in Mexico where Nahuatl, the ancient Aztec language, is by far the dominant tongue. As a renowned teacher of Nahuatl, he was featured on local television and the Public Broadcasting System.

And the church was often filled with an extensive Belizean family, descended from people who had been taken to the Caribbean as slaves. They found a warm welcome at Messiah. I remember several funerals where the male family members would insist on interring the casket themselves, digging with hand-shovels, while the women stood in the shade of the trees singing gospel hymns.

So, all this is to say that I have for years enjoyed a deep connection to the spirituality of indigenous and immigrant people. I have experienced the profound passion which pervades spirituality and daily life, where one becomes the other—where spirituality and daily life cannot be separated. I believe that this experience fostered in me an intuitive interest in and an appreciation for the Native American tribal and Hispano traditions which I continue to encounter in the Southwest, and which I describe in this book.

Desert Spirit Places

I will also share some reflections from my philosophy classes at Saddleback Community College, Mission Viejo, California, where I have been an instructor since 1973. We will be able to look at desert spirituality and the Sacred in general, in the context of some of the philosophers who speak to our modern, secular minds: René Descartes, Blaise Pascal, Thomas Merton and Charles Taylor.

As I say to my students in the first lecture of the semester, I know that there is a chronic restlessness, a dissatisfaction and a longing in our hearts that neither possessions, nor other people, nor peak life experiences can address. Father Ron Rolheiser writes:

> We are forever restless, dissatisfied, frustrated and aching. We are so overcharged with desire that it is hard to simply rest . . . We are driven persons, forever obsessed, congenitally dis-eased, living lives of quiet desperation.[2]

How we respond to these desires and passions is our Spirituality.

Spirituality is about how I find love, hope, peace and joy in a world of distractions and enticements. My promise to my students is always that if they journey with me with open hearts over the seventeen weeks of classroom lectures, reflection and outside exploration, they will find resources that will enrich and underpin their personal spirituality. However, I also warn them that Euro-American culture has been inoculated with suspicion and dismissiveness of personal spiritual experiences, and indeed anything that smacks of mysticism.

The old world of my Latino and Belizean parishioners, their animistic rituals and traditions, has been displaced by a modern world of reason and science. The disenchantment of this modern world was sparked by René Descartes, who counseled that the best antidote to the encroachment of the old superstitions was a "buffered self." The Canadian philosopher Charles Taylor writes:

> The buffered self is the agent who no longer fears demons, spirits and magic forces. More radically, these no longer impinge; they don't exist for him; whatever threat or other meaning they proffer doesn't "get it" from him.
>
> The super buffered self . . . is not only not "got at" by demons and spirits; he is also unmoved by the aura of desire. In a mechanistic universe, and in a field of functionally understood passion, there

---

2. Rolheiser, *Holy Longing*, 8.

Cedar Mesa, Utah—By Way of Introduction

is no more room for such an aura. There is nothing it could correspond to. It is just a disturbing, supercharged feeling, which somehow grips us until we can come to our senses, and take on our full, buffered identity.[3]

As you and I go into the desert spirit places of the American Southwest, we must acknowledge that we have been tutored, consciously or not, by this buffered self to keep a firewall between our heads and our hearts. And yet, as we encounter Native American tribal and Hispano cultures and their porous sensitivity to the Sacred, that inner restlessness and gnawing dissatisfaction still rummages about within us. We keep a safe distance, take photographs, ask too many questions. The dancing and singing we witness at ceremonials are perceived as cultural expression rather than deeply felt prayer to the Holy.

For all that, I believe that porous sensitivity to the Sacred and our longing for communion with the Holy have not entirely left us. The wonder and gift of experiencing desert spirit places can be like the persistent grains of sand that wear down a boulder of granite. All it takes is a breeze and time and eventually the shape will change. Through time, I believe, the Sacred reshapes us. That is the gift of these desert spirit places—a gift for the taking.

In conversations with readers of my previous books, I hear a deep longing for encounters with the Sacred; not so much the collecting of "peak experiences," but the search for life-changing encounters, metanoia. As St. Ignatius Loyola would encourage, we may find ourselves visited by deeply felt spiritual realities that awaken an awareness of the Benevolent Presence of peace and joy. Although the sensations of that direct encounter with the Holy may be ephemeral, the memory remains. Ignatius calls this memory a foundational experience of the Holy, which we can revisit in our prayer and meditation.

The deserts of the American Southwest will be the backdrop for our exploration of life behind the buffered self. Philip Ferranti, who gives seminars on personal transformation, refers to the Southwest as a "fusion of spiritual history and spiritual geography, resulting in a spirituality of place." In a survey he conducted, 95 percent of respondents sought the desert as the preferred setting for the exploration of the inner self.

---

3. Taylor, *Secular Age*, 135–36.

I am lying on a cold, steel slab which is covered with a thin cotton pad. My legs are confined by a molded form. I cross my arms over my chest and close my eyes. The ultrasound machine checks the positioning of my body and that my bladder is completely full (oh, that does hurt!). I hear the linear accelerator warming up and beginning to slowly rotate around my body. The machine will irradiate my prostate from all points of the compass. I have high-grade prostate cancer. This is the first of forty-five days of treatment. My body slides into the tube of the linear accelerator but my mind takes the journey back to a foundational desert experience.

I am standing with my wife and son at a split-rail fence on a bluff outside Goulding's Trading Post in Monument Valley, Utah. A full moon rises over the iconic mesas. Moonlight over landscape. The night is quiet and I am aware of the holy embrace of a Benevolent Presence. I remember that desert spirit place as the nuclear machine attacks the tumors and I pray for healing.

May this book invite you into other desert spirit places! May you find yourself open to the gifts and blessings that await you there!

2.

Grand Canyon, Arizona
—Living on Bread and Water

> We used to climb a little hill at the end of the day, all the work done, and look out over the land and just feel good to be alive.
> —Lemuel Paya[1]

THE SWIRLING CLOUD OF fine, red volcanic dust heaves into the sky in an immense crimson tornado, obscuring the dangerous edge of the Grand Canyon mesa, which drops off three thousand feet to the Colorado River below. The helicopter rotors slow and stop. The dust cloud dissipates as my father and the Havasupai pilot emerge.

It is September 1972. My father, Lyle Karelius, has arrived as a field engineer for Thompson Concrete Pumps, a division of Royal Industries. Two weeks ago, he was in the high mountains of Bolivia, consulting at a silver mine. He will spend the next ten days working on a water project at the bottom of Havasu Canyon, in one of the most isolated Native American reservations.

Water is life for these First People who have lived in this area for almost a millennium. The Havasupai were not originally canyon dwellers. Their ancestral lands were on the plateau of the south rim of the Grand Canyon, extending as far as Flagstaff and Williams, Arizona. It is an old story: silver miners and railroad barons displaced the tribe and the US Government established a tiny reservation. As the Grand Canyon National

---

1. Paya (quoted), *Life in a Narrow Place*, xiii.

Park developed, the National Park Service took more of the native plateau lands, hemming the tribe into the narrow canyon.

Nowadays, the tribe is financially dependent on the twenty thousand visitors who each year hike a ten-mile trail to the famous blue-green waters of Havasupai Falls. The tourist destination has become so popular it is almost impossible to secure a reservation without going through a tour company. But what is gorgeous in spring and summer turns dreary and sometimes dangerous at the end of the year.

Havasu Falls, 2007. Photo by Gonzo fan.

> The canyon that the summer visitors view as a landlocked Polynesia, the Havasupai viewed in winter as a prison. The lack of winter sunlight stops all agriculture from November to March, and the canyon turns from a lush oasis to a barren place of confinement.[2]

My father tells me how he peered over the edge of the Grand Canyon at Hualapai hilltop, looking for the village of Supai. The pilot guided my father's vision to a faint smudge of green. This is where they would go in the helicopter to assess the suitability of the construction site for concrete-encased pipes and a cistern.

For six hundred years the Havasupai had constructed *ha ya gewa* ditches that ran on both sides of the creek. They need the water to grow

---

2 Paya, *Life in a Narrow Place*, 8.

Grand Canyon, Arizona — Living on Bread and Water

corn, squash and beans and to irrigate clusters of fruit trees. This plan had worked for centuries, but by the early 1970s the dominant Anglo powers on the plateau above had created complicated rules about water storage that made water less available to the tribe. Then drought hit—*years* of drought. My father's work on the new water project would help to conserve water during drought, and also the concrete-encased pipes and cistern would be less vulnerable than the *ha ya gewa* to the powerful, life-erasing flash floods that periodically thunder through the narrow canyon.

For the next two weeks, lines of concrete-laden trucks drove down Route 66, then on to the dusty desert Bureau of Indian Affairs Road 18, to Hualapai hilltop. Two helicopters were used to lift buckets of wet concrete suspended on long cables, rotating back and forth from the Grand Canyon plateau to the Supai village, three thousand feed below. A photo of my father shows his bald head and face streaked with wet grey concrete. He was smiling. He was alive, living in his element. The Indian workers bantered in their native Havasupai-Hualapai. Bottles of Coca-Cola glistened in ice-packed metal tubs next to a mound of cold watermelon—enticing gifts from the helicopters.

My father remembers the day of completion. A Havasupai shaman blessed the new pipe system with burning sage bundles and tobacco. A signal fire was lit in the village and workers on the plateau above opened the control valve. The water flowed with a creaking, thunderous roar through cast iron pipes from above to the cistern and pipes below.

In 2013, when he was ninety-five, my father shared this memory with me. Although short-term memories challenged him, his recall of this grand project of forty years ago was vivid and sharply detailed. As he described his experience, his eyes were dancing, his hands gesturing energetically, his face filled with delight.

The fight for water rights continues. In 2017, an intense court battle negated a Havasupai lawsuit over commercial pumping of groundwater reserves.

Over thirty books have been written on this isolated tribe of Native Americans. I was surprised to find another personal connection to them when I discovered that my Episcopal Church has had a mission to this tribe since 1923. And has the mission followed that worn and unsavory script: conversion to Christianity entailing the suppression of the extant religious traditions and culture?

In fact, this has not been the case. More than anything, the Episcopal mission has succeeded through building relationships of friendship and trust. Some of this involved bringing assistance for education and nutrition, and equally, if not more importantly, because the Episcopal Church has long been deeply involved in social justice and advocacy for civil rights, it was well-prepared to be a key advocate for the tribe in the early 1970s for the return of 93,000 acres from the US Government. The land was given back in 1975.

Havasupai Indian School, Cataract Canyon. 1901. Photo by Henry G. Peabody. Library of Congress, Prints and Photographs Division, reproduction LC-USZ262-112672.

I found a copy of *Life Magazine*, dated July 15, 1946. Bishop Arthur B. Kinsolving, Episcopal bishop of Arizona, rides horseback down a dangerous, rocky trail into Cataract Canyon of the Havasupai. It was the bishop's annual visitation for baptism and confirmation. His old friend Chief Big Jim would be confirmed at the age of one hundred. The old Havasupai religious traditions coexisted alongside Episcopal spirituality. Chief Big Jim saw in an image of Jesus a similarity to the native god, Bagaviova.

In the shadow of the landmark El Tovar Hotel, at the very edge of the Grand Canyon's south rim, stands of pinyon pines belt the parking lots with

Grand Canyon, Arizona — Living on Bread and Water

green. My wife, Jan, and I and our son, Erik, walk in the cool of the trees to our truck. We are not chatting and joking as when we had started out, because we are tired after a two-hour hike along the rim, but we are also still held breathless by the vast beauty about and below us. As we are settling in our seats, I spot a large, fleshy woman in an outsize Northern Arizona University sweatshirt—she is bent over, moving with careful intent, searching beneath the pines. Has she lost something? Ah, then it occurs to me; the month is October; these are pinyon trees. She is a Native American and she is looking for fallen seeds.

I get down from the truck and walk gingerly over to her. Jan joins me. I wish the lady a good afternoon and ask whether she is looking for pinyon seeds. She straightens up and looks at me with the smile of shared knowledge. "Yes," she says, and holds up a half-filled sandwich bag.

"How do you know where the seeds are?" asks Jan.

"It does take a while for your eyes to adjust . . . See, here's one."

Jan kneels down beside the woman. It turns out that Jan is pretty good at seed-gathering, for after fifteen quiet minutes she has a good handful to add to the sandwich bag. I join the women and find that you need very sharp eyes for this task: you are looking for dark pearls against dark, dense pine needles, in the shade.

I ask our new acquaintance if she lives nearby. "Yes," she says, "My people are the Havasupai. We live in Cataract Canyon in the Grand Canyon, but it is too cold for me down there in the winter, so my family moves up here."

I shared with her the story of my father's work on the Havasuapi water project, many years ago. He engineered the project that poured concrete for a reservoir and irrigation system on land that had just been won back from the Federal Government after tortuous negotiations. The concrete had to be brought down to Cataract Canyon in great buckets slung under helicopters. There was no way to pump or walk-in concrete eight miles from the road! The woman remembered this; she was a little girl then, and it was the first time she had seen such noisy mechanical birds.

Then I was recalling the chapter on pinyon pine that I had written in my previous book: about how the pinyon seed or nut was a primary source of calories and fat and protein for the Paiute people of the Owens Valley, how there were different ways of harvesting the seeds, and how the shaman would be able to tell months ahead whether it would be a good year or a lean year. Ronald Lanner wrote an entire book extolling the tree and its fruit.

> The little tree produced the fuel, building materials, food and medicines that enabled prehistoric Indians to establish their cultures on the Colorado Plateau—and to survive into the present as Hopi, Zuni, Pueblo and Navajo. It was the pinyon that made the Great Basin the coarse-grained Eden of the pine-nut eaters who picked their winter sustenance from the treetops.[3]

I asked our friend, "Do you still pull down the green pine cones and roast them and shake out the nuts into a blanket?" She said that that is certainly what she had done all her life but that her children and grandchildren had drifted away from these traditions. So here she is, searching for pinyon nuts on the median strip, surrounded by hundreds of tourist cars. Mother Earth continues to feed her.

As we helped fill her bag, she would now and then crunch a seed between her teeth. "They taste better roasted," she said. But the look on her face was one of holy pleasure. For her these seeds are manna, sacred sustenance and communion with her ancestors.

Driving back to Williams, where we had left our RV trailer, I thought about this lady gathering her pinyon, manna, bread of heaven. My mind drifted to the endless, frightening wilderness of the Sinai over three thousand years ago. God had freed the Hebrew people from slavery, but then they had wandered for years in the desert, years in which they were entirely dependent on God for food and water. One of the foods that miraculously appeared was called manna.

The Book of Exodus describes manna as being of the color of white coriander seeds. It would appear as dew in the morning and had to be collected before it melted in the sun. The Book of Numbers tells us how manna was baked into cakes. It tasted like wafers made with honey. Manna could not be gathered and stored since it spoiled quickly, so each day a supply of manna had to be gathered anew, each day the Hebrews found themselves once again dependent on the grace of God. We don't know exactly what manna was or is, but I read somewhere that it might have been the sweet and aromatic secretion of the tamarisk tree.

The Holy Qu'ran mentions manna three times. In the *Hadith*, the collection of commentary and sayings of Mohammed, it is said, "Truffles are

---

3. Lanner, *Piñon Pine*, 8.

part of the 'manna' which Allah sent to the people of Israel through Moses, and its juice is a medicine for the eyes."[4]

Because we humans are forgetful of blessings, the Torah of God commands the Hebrew people to remember what happened in the Sinai wilderness and how they were led there, by every year celebrating a commemorative meal called the Seder, the Passover Meal. During the meal, the story is told of how the Angel of Death passed over the houses of the people of Israel when they were still in Egypt, and how they were liberated from slavery. The Haggadah is the written instruction that lays out the ritual of the Seder and the telling of the Passover story, for use in the Jewish home. Most of the time the Hebrew verbs are in the past tense, remembering, but at a certain point the verbs are put in the present tense so that those who participate in the Seder today are transported in time and space to share in the exact event of the Exodus.

On Holy Thursday, Jesus gathered his disciples together to celebrate this sacred meal. Knowing that his suffering and death were near, he took the unleavened bread and the wine into his hands and he told them, "This is my Body. This is my Blood." He said that whenever they gather in his name to share this meal, he would be present with them. After the Resurrection of Jesus a few days later, the community of disciples was galvanized by the fulfillment of Jesus' promise that he would be always with them.

Since the earliest days of Christianity, followers of Jesus have gathered to celebrate this part of the Seder meal, where they express in the present tense the Real Presence of Jesus in the bread and wine.

I am writing this after attending Sunday evening mass at St. Timothy Roman Catholic Church in Laguna Niguel, California. Now that I am retired after all my years as an Episcopal priest, and especially those thirty spent as pastor in Santa Ana with that richly textured, vibrant, multicultural congregation, I have not been able to reduplicate the experience in another Episcopal congregation nearby. When I am not filling in for a priest on vacation, our family attends the Sunday evening youth Mass at St. Timothy's, a few blocks from home. There is a rule in most Roman Catholic dioceses that inhibits non-Romans from receiving Communion. However, I have to share this with you: at the time of Communion I am almost always overwhelmed by the powerful embrace of the Holy Spirit. It squeezes me so tight that I must work really hard to hold back the tears of joy.

---

4. Muslim, *Sahih Muslim*, book 23:5084.

I realize that as a follower of Jesus I hunger for this eucharistic manna; it keeps me alive. Even when I do not physically receive the sacrament, I am being nourished by this daily manna. Even then, my family and I are blessed with another day in the desert of our lives.

In chapter 6 of the Gospel of John, Jesus says, "Unless you eat the bread of life, you will not have life within you." Saint John links this bread of heaven, the body of Christ, to the daily nourishment that the Hebrew people received from God in their desert years. I am told that when the manna was combined with food that came from Egypt, it tasted bitter. When manna alone was eaten, it was sweet.

There is a tradition among Orthodox Christians, Roman Catholics and some Anglicans of daily Eucharist. It is a spiritual discipline that allows us to receive God's embrace as often as Israel in the wilderness. The ritual of the scripture readings, prayers and Communion is life-giving: a daily gathering around the Word and the Sacrament. It transforms us, I believe, so that we ourselves can be manna for the world.

Almost every night our family comes together for dinner in our home. We begin the meal with grace, thanksgiving for the day and petitions for those in need. We share our simple meal and talk about how the day went. These rhythms and rituals of coming together, praying, eating and sharing are part of what makes us a family. Just as the Church offers us this daily manna, we need the daily manna of being present to each other.

3.

From Lone Pine, California, to the Valley of the Kings —The Curse of the Dust Devils

> Here you find the hot sink of Death Valley, or high rolling districts where the air has always a tang of frost. Here are the long heavy winds and breathless calms on the tilted mesas where the dust devils dance, whirling up into a wide, pale sky. Here you have no rain when the earth cries for it, or quick downpours called cloudbursts for violence. A land of lost rivers, with little in it to love; yet a land that once visited, must be come back to inevitably. If it were not so, there would be little told of it.
> —Mary Austin[1]

THE HOT AUGUST SUN sets behind the Sierra Nevada as I walk a dusty trail towards the faded-yellow Southern Pacific Railroad station. It lies off Narrow Gauge Road, north of Lone Pine. Dry, still desert air suddenly takes on a brisk breeze. Ahead looms a smudgy brown swirling cloud. This is a dust devil. Many times have I seen and felt these turbulent little twisters spin across the highway and shake my car. This time I have no protection and the dust devil is headed directly towards me. Nowhere to turn. Nowhere to hide. I kneel down on the trail, tug my shirt over my mouth and nose, cover my head with my arms, and wait.

The wind rushes in my ears. I am pelted with thousands of sand granules. That is the preliminaries. Closer . . . closer. Now the devil envelopes me. It covers me like a heavy, billowing blanket. I can't avoid taking the dust into my lungs. Then, after just a couple of minutes it is gone, dancing on

---

1. Austin, *Land of Little Rain*, 8.

its capricious way, leaving me feeling like a horned-toad covered in desert siftings. The air is still again. That was an experience!

The Sinagua Indians of Arizona call dust devils Siwulogi. The word is pronounced in a respectful whisper. Siwulogi are believed to be evil spirits that emerge from underground. When they see a whirling in the distance, the Sinagua remove their hats and place them on the ground between themselves and the dust devil. My Latino parishioners use the name remolinos. (swirls, confusion). The twisting clouds are to be respected by making the Sign of the Cross in their direction. Carmen Villa Prezelski writes about Latino culture for the *Tucson Citizen*. She quotes:

> My dad always said dust devils came up because the devil was moving around down underground, causing a commotion. That's why they formed the cross.[2]

Dust devil in Arizona. 2005. NASA photo.

2. Allen, *Tucson Citizen*, July 3, 1996.

Dust devils occur throughout the Southwestern desert places and have other names too, such as the "dancing devil," and in Death Valley they may be called "sand augers" or "dust whirls."

Anthropologist James Mooney recorded the Paiute "Songs of Life Returning," expressing the spiritual potency of these erratic desert winds:

> There is a dust from the whirlwind
> There is a dust from the whirlwind
> The whirlwind on the mountain.

And the historical geographer Richard Francaviglia has this to say on the subject:

> ... dust devils are a manifestation of spirits who endlessly stalk the earth in search of the unfortunate. They rob a person of spiritual strength, and such weakening exposes individuals to illness and misfortune.[3]

The Bible has twenty-two passages relating to the spiritual power of the whirlwind. The most important are:

> Job 38:1 – Then the Lord answered Job out of the whirlwind ...

> Psalm 77:18 – The sound of Your Thunder was in the whirlwind; the lightnings lit up the world; the earth trembled and shook.

> 2 Kings 2:11 – As they were going along and talking, behold, there appeared a chariot of fire and horses of fire which separated the two of them. And Elijah went up by a whirlwind to heaven.

In contrasting the Judeo-Christian-Islamic orientation toward desert winds with Native American spirituality, William Least Heat Moon observes:

> ... people of the Old Testament heard the voice of God in desert whirlwinds, but Southwestern Indians saw evil spirits in the spumes and sang aloud if one crossed their path.[4]

Among the Navajo, dust devils have an ominous presence as *chindi*, or the ghosts of dead Diné. It is a good spirit if it spins clockwise; an evil spirit if it spins counterclockwise. I can tell you from personal experience that when you are caught in the midst of one, there is no way of knowing

---

3. Francaviglia, *Believing in Place*, 82.
4. Moon, *Blue Highways*, 156.

which way the wind turns. It grabs you from all directions, stinging and blinding you.

There is one positive and surprising story of a Navajo/Diné encounter with a dust devil, as told by Michael Sean Comerford:

> Navajo Mike's mother and grandmother say he was just a year old when a dust devil drew him up into the air and above their grasp "for about 600 feet." They ran after him, trying to pull him back before, "it dropped me down into their arms," he says on a video I took of him while he was driving.
>
> He clearly thinks it means he is something special, nature knew it and showed it by lifting him up in a dust devil. Now, when he sees dust devils—and he sees them often in this part of the world—he thinks about what I meant. What was that all about? What is this life all about?[5]

Paul Sinclair of Colorado State University has shown that dust devils can reach a height of two thousand feet and move at a rate of up to forty miles per hour. They have been known to turn over cars and small airplanes.

After my hair-raising experience, I actually felt fine. Little did I know that the Curse would take its time in possessing me! Two months later, in October, the change set in: I became increasingly fatigued, felt weaker and weaker, my joints ached, night sweats set in, I could hardly lift my head from the pillow, it felt like someone was trying to choke me all the time.

Off I went to see my internist, Dr. James Sperber, who ran all sorts of tests looking for brain tumors, lung cancer, leukemia—a grim list, and fortunately there was nothing of the sort. With characteristic thoroughness, Dr. Jim remembered someone he had treated earlier with similar symptoms. He rechecked my bloodwork and came up with the hypothesis that I was suffering from coccidioidomycosis—valley fever. Cocci is a fungal disease common in desert climates. Microscopic spores proliferate in the dusty soil and when the wind stirs them, they readily land in the moist lung tissue. The disease was first identified in the San Joaquin Valley and is becoming increasingly common in California and Arizona. About 150 people die from the disease each year; the biggest problem is that, untreated, the spores can cause perforations in the lungs. Coccidioidomycosis can literally possess your body with debilitating consequences, often quickly ending your life.

---

5. Comerford, "Incredible Story of Navajo Mike."

Perhaps valley fever was the legendary curse of King Tutankhamen's tomb. Several members of archaeologist Howard Carter's team, who in 1923 entered the sealed doorway of the king's resting place—undisturbed for over three millennia—succumbed to mysterious diseases. After the tomb's excavation and cataloging, a text was found that warned of dire punishment befalling anyone who violated the royal burial chamber. Some medical experts suggest that the deathly curse came from a long-dormant fungus like coccidioidomycosis, lying in the dust amongst the regal relics.

Dr. Jim prescribed for me a common antifungal medication, Diflucan. Within two days I was up and mowing the front lawn. A profound respect for the mysterious dust devil has never left me.

4.

El Sanctuario de Chimayo, New Mexico — Holy Healing

> In the middle of the earthen floor is a small hole, about the right size for planting some flowers. Somewhat incongruously, into the hole were stuck three brightly colored plastic shovels, like those a child would use at the seashore.
>
> —James Martin, SJ[1]

THE ROAD TO EL Sanctuario de Chimayo winds through ancient country in northern New Mexico, passing through Native American pueblos and Hispano hamlets. Janice, Erik and I are midway through our vacation and we join other pilgrims who are making the journey to the most visited Catholic shrine in the United States. There is the renowned Chapel of Healing Sands somewhere up there. I am told that during Lent, and especially on Good Friday, pilgrims will walk to the chapel from as far away as Albuquerque—some ninety miles. As we drive, we pass a bearded Latino man with a backpack—a pilgrim perhaps?

On Good Friday in 1810, Don Bernardo Abeyta was praying the Stations of the Cross, meditating on top of one of the hills near his rancho, when he noticed something odd buried in the dirt. It turned out to be an antique crucifix. You can see the holy relic on the altar of the Chapel of Healing Sands today, and the exact place where the rancher found it is called the Pit of the Holy Dirt—such a strange name! But people from all over the United States come here with hopes of healing, as here they meet

---

1. Martin, "Holy Dirt."

El Sanctuario de Chimayo, New Mexico — Holy Healing

Jesus in his Passion and suffering for humankind. A visitor put her feelings succinctly, "This is a place where you feel the suffering of Jesus and other people."

We park in the vast parking lot; there is plenty of room for the buses full of pilgrims. The day of our visit was the Feast of St. Francis and I thought there would be a crowd, but as it happened the feast was translated to the following day, a Saturday, so there were not too many people when we arrived mid-afternoon.

We climbed a long wheelchair ramp, water gurgled in a nearby brook, wind rustled the golden leaves of cottonwood and aspen. Autumn was gently transforming the mountain landscape. We passed other pilgrims leaving the shrine and they smiled at Erik. There is a marked welcoming attitude toward the sick and disabled in this place of healing. On a rock wall beside the brook, pilgrims had secured wooden crosses with the names of deceased loved ones.

Erik and I entered the sanctuary. We sat in the front pew surrounded by a dazzlingly colorful array of folk-art: carvings of holy figures or Santos and wall decorations. We said our prayers and got up to begin exploring. We were going to find the Chapel of the Healing Sand. I left Erik with Jan for a few minutes and went to try a side-door—and sure enough it opened into a holy space, for along the walls were hung crutches and other orthopedic devices, presumably left there by people who no longer needed them. A large poster was pasted with photos of visitors. Had each of these received some kind of healing blessing?

I went in further and there was another door, much smaller, and I had to bow to get through it. In the middle of the floor was a hole about two feet wide and two feet deep, filled with sand. There was a man stationed there who welcomed me to the Place of Holy Sand, telling me his story of how he had been depressed to the point of suicide some years ago and came to this place, took some of the holy sand home and placed it under his bed. The following morning he awoke with a new spirit of hope and an inner voice that called him to minister to others who come to this place. Apparently, he has some sanction from the parish priest and has become a semi-official host. After some conversation I went to find Jan and Erik and suggested that they go into the Place of the Holy Sand too.

After about a half-hour they returned to me in the chapel courtyard, where I was minding our dog. In Jan's own words, here is what she experienced with Erik.

On a lovely autumn day, Brad, Erik, and I drove from Santa Fe in northern New Mexico along a long winding country road to Santuario de Chimayo, called the Place of Holy Sand. It had apparently been a "place of the spirit" to the Native Americans long before the Spanish visited the area, so it had a long spiritual history. A long time ago, a farmer dug up an old Spanish cross in the exact place where stories of miraculous healing happened and they built the church next to that place. Chimayo is one of the most visited Roman Catholic pilgrimage sites in North America. In fact, we saw several people with backpacks traveling along the narrow back-country road and we wondered whether they were on a spiritual journey to Chimayo.

Author with Erik Karelius at Sanctuario de Chimayo. 2014. Photo by Janice Karelius.

El Sanctuario de Chimayo, New Mexico—Holy Healing

We finally arrived at a very old, tiny village with two churches and a few scattered buildings on a dirt road. We drove behind the Santuario de Chimayo to a surprisingly large parking lot near a running stream and walked up a long wheelchair ramp to the front of an old church courtyard containing timeworn grave stones, crosses and a few family monuments. Standing back looking down on the scene, I was struck by the old church surrounded by equally old trees in full autumn glory of yellow, bright orange, mixed with green. There was a feeling of reverence to the scene, and I noticed the warm smiles from people who passed us, many of whom appeared sick and lame. I spoke to a few people in the courtyard while waiting for Brad and Erik to return from visiting inside the church. Most of the visitors came for healing or to express gratitude for healing.

Eventually, Erik and I made our way to a small long, narrow, dark annex beside the church. The passage was filled with various assistive devices; walkers, crutches, canes, even a wheelchair. All over the walls were posters filled with pictures and messages from those who were ill and needed prayers or healing. We slowly walked toward a small room with a low door where we were met by a man with whom I had spoken earlier. At Chimayo he had found relief from serious chronic depression and now he had a sense of purpose to guide others in their experience of this holy place. There were also two other people who warmly greeted Erik and looked at him with deep concern. Erik said hello and shook their hands before we bent our heads to enter a small room filled with *ofrendas* (ritual objects placed on an altar), the walls were covered with holy medals, rosary beads, small statues, and mementos left by other visitors. In the candlelight, I saw a hole in the center of the room, about two feet around and two feet deep.

Erik was directed to step into the hole and I held him steady so he would not trip and fall. The attendant asked me to tell them about Erik, so I said he had suffered an infection in his brain when he was four years old that left him with brain damage and frequent seizures. I explained that during his childhood, he was very ill and close to death many times, but he had survived to be quite healthy and to have a good life, surrounded by loving family and many friends. As I talked about the gifts Erik has received, accepting people at face value, living completely in the present moment without fear or anxiety, trusting that he is safe with us, even during difficult medical procedures, the sad and concerned faces of the three people became joyful as they rubbed his shoulder or held his hand while I was talking.

Erik was listening to the conversation, and continued to stand in the hole of sand without moving, giving himself over to the gentle stroking and smiling faces. He looked very peaceful so I asked him if he liked this quiet place. He replied, "I like it!" smiling at the people around him.

We laid hands on him in the little hole of sand while offering prayers for his continued healing in gratitude for his health and happiness with his family. The feeling of peace and joy in the room was palpable. We continued to stand quietly together for a few minutes in that well prayed-in place, until Erik stepped from the hole. Before we left, the attendant took a shovel and filled a plastic bag with some of the sand for me to bring home to share.

I still have some of the sand, though over time the amount has diminished as we have given it away to various people who are in need of the healing sand and the peace of Chimayo.

Sanctuario de Chimayo, Chapel of the Healing Sand. 2014. Photo by author.

El Sanctuario de Chimayo, New Mexico—Holy Healing

Janice and I respectfully joked that after this event, Erik, who is mentally three or four years old, was now able to do simple multiplication. Of course, that was not true. However, our family could sense a holy presence there in the Chapel of the Holy Sand. We remember the many years of Erik's hospitalizations and his great physical suffering. Things have stabilized for him now and we are less anxious and more grateful for every day we have with him. He was a wonderful, receptive traveler on that vacation journey and during our little pilgrimage, when of course Erik had our undivided attention. The day of our little pilgrimage was mild, with all the scents and colors of autumn. It could not have been more delightful—and healing. Four days after our visit, it snowed up there!

And the bag of sand that the host gave to Jan to share back home? People rub the sand into the parts of their bodies that are afflicted as they pray for healing. Apparently, over these two hundred years, something has been going on because people continue to make the pilgrimage to Chimayo for healing.

Holy Week 1995. I am frantically busy, planning the details of fifteen different masses and liturgies. Erik is sitting at the breakfast table eating his oatmeal. I notice something: "Jan, Erik's left eye is red and all puffy. What do you think that means?" My wife, the family nurse-practitioner, looks carefully at the eye and says, "Uh-oh. Trouble." The herpes in his eye that was connected to his catastrophic encephalitis back in 1987 seemed to be reactivated. After an emergency visit to his pediatrician, we drove up to the USC Doheny Eye Clinic in Los Angeles for an appointment with the clinic head, Dr. Rao. Erik needed intravenous Acyclovir as immediate intervention, because the retina in his left eye had become detached, which could blind him. Erik's health can take a drastic turn for the worse faster than you can snap your fingers. Dr. Rao wanted to put Erik in the hospital for the infusions, but Jan said we would do this at home. It meant treatment every six hours, hanging an IV bag from a wooden step-ladder.

My concerns about planning for Holy Week quickly faded into the background. Erik was now undergoing his own Passion: patiently allowing Jan to prick and probe his skin and to apply many eye ointments over two weeks of intensive treatment at home. What a trooper he was and is!

Then we returned to the Doheny Clinic. Dr. Rao carefully looked into Erik's eyes with his complex scopes. "How does the retina get reattached, if it disconnects?" I asked, man of many questions.

"Surgery." Replied the doctor. "It is like sewing very thin Saran Wrap. Doesn't always work." Now he was very quiet. I need to shut up and wait. He goes off to a corner, rubs his chin. "This is very curious. The retina has reattached on its own. I don't think I have ever seen anything like this."

"How could that happen?" I ask.

He looks at me, smiles and says, "You are the priest, aren't you? You should be telling me!"

I began seminary in Berkeley in 1967. Over those three years, tumultuous years in that city and throughout the United States, I studied scripture, theology, and pastoral care. The rational, skeptical, buffered mind (about which a lot more, later) was cultivated, plumbing the depths of Christian thought and doctrine. I entered seminary full of passion and love for God. I graduated, having cultivated academic knowledge, supposedly prepared for parish ministry.

At my first parish, St. Mary's, Laguna Beach, we had a healing mass every Thursday. Parishioners came to the altar-rail for anointing, for healing for themselves and others. I went through the motions with sincerity, but did I actually believe that God heals?

Over these forty-three years as a priest, I have anointed hundreds of people with blessed oil, praying persons through surgeries, chemotherapy, and in the last breath of life. I am grateful that God's Amazing Grace has softened those skeptical spirits within me, as the sick and dying have held my hand, and their spirits have infused me with their faith, and the Passion of Jesus on the Cross has enfolded all of us with the hope of ultimate healing, wholeness and resurrection.

And what do I personally believe about prayer and healing?

My Christian tradition has held the bedrock belief that somewhere within sickness there is a sin, known or unknown, that is related to the sickness. In the old English Book of Common Prayer, the ritual of the Ministry to the Sick includes confession with the priest and a prayer that is along the lines of asking God to stay His wrath and to bring healing. In my study of world religions I see that most spiritual traditions have a sense of dis-ease as a painful symptom of something that is out of harmony and balance. A professional healer is called in to restore balance.

I don't believe God causes sickness, but nonetheless there is a dark spirit that prods me with this thought: maybe Erik's sickness or my own sickness is because of something I did. I dismiss that voice.

El Sanctuario de Chimayo, New Mexico — Holy Healing

I live within a family of professional healers: Jan is the family nurse-practitioner who worked for forty-five years in the emergency room at Mission Hospital, Laguna Beach. Our daughter, Katie, has been a hospital oncology nurse and nurse case-manager for a hospice company. Our dinner-table conversation is often about current cases of the sick and dying. I listen to clinical voices reviewing organic causes and effects. As I hear the conversation and read media reports about new discoveries of medication and treatment, there is a sense that science is moving forward to cure disease.

Where is the God of my faith? I look back on Erik's long medical history and the evolving clinical tools for treatment and medication. Our family lives in a world of privilege with access to the best resources. If we were living in a less privileged context, here in America or in another country, Erik certainly would have died years ago.

Two thoughts come to me.

First, how my friend Rabbi Harold Kushner paraphrased Martin Buber: "When bad things happen to good people, where is God? Look around you for the people God sends to you in the times of sickness, suffering, and dying. People are God's language." This counsel has sparked a heightened awareness of the people who have come into our life during Erik's crises.

Second, I must remember the past encounters with Amazing Grace, when we were at the end of our resources, fatigued, on our knees attending to Erik's great suffering, darkness encroaching upon us. Always a door opened, a resource appeared, or there was a brief recovery, a respite. I do not believe God is manipulating the scenario, but I must look back and remember in gratitude all those times of grace.

As another friend, Father Gordon Moreland SJ, counseled: "Hope without gratitude is wishful thinking. Gratitude is foundational to hope."

September 2016. After tests and scans at Cedars Sinai Hospital in Los Angeles, I was diagnosed with high-grade prostate cancer. The good news was that the scans did not show that the cancer had spread. But I can still imagine little cancer cells moving around in my body looking for somewhere to grow. The treatment is forty-five days of radiation and two years of chemotherapy with Lupron.

My father died at the age of ninety-nine. This diagnosis of cancer erased my fantasy of a long life.

The day before I was to begin daily radiation with a linear accelerator, hitting the tumors from 360 degrees, I visited my friend, Monsignor John Urell at St. Timothy Parish, Laguna Niguel, California. We went into the chapel and he anointed me with blessed oil. The prayers for healing are the same as the prayers for the dying. I have prayed these prayers with my own parishioners for forty-five years. Then, as I lay on the cold metal slab at oncology radiology, I crossed my arms, closed my eyes and my imagination went back to the desert, remembering with gratitude God's presence bringing Grace in difficult times.

My most significant memory of God's healing presence is the memory of bringing weekly communion to the home of Chad DeLeeuw in 1988, when he was slowly dying of AIDS. Each visit presented a human form, more thin and weak and wasted from the last visit. But his hunger for the Eucharist and my prayers were strong. Breath labored, he would pray the Confession and Lord's Prayer very slowly. Chad was experiencing his own Passion, but his heart and eyes were looking East toward his Resurrection and ultimate wholeness with the Lord. I brought him the love of a Church that cherished and blessed him, just as God had created him.

Jan mentioned above that we have been distributing the Holy Sand among our sick friends and the supply at our home is becoming depleted. The time is coming when we must visit El Sanctuario de Chimayo again.

Zuni Indian bead worker. 1903. Photo by Edward S. Curtis. Author's Collection. Library of Congress, Prints and Photographs Division, reproduction LC-USZ6257.

5.

Zuni Pueblo, New Mexico
—Zuni Fetish: Living Stones

> You have to want to come here. Our visitors tend to be better educated and more culturally aware. Their reward is often a very profound experience.
> —Roger Thomas, owner of the Inn at Halona[1]

IT IS 1540. IN the distance, silver helmets and breastplates reflect the brilliant July sun as Spanish soldiers mounted on majestic Lipizzaner stallions march toward me in a swirling cloud of dust. Franciscan monks carry crosses and the flag of Spain. Francisco Vazquez de Coronado y Lujan is leading the desert procession. He is searching for the legendary Seven Cities of Cibola. This is how he comes upon the Zuni homeland of Shiwannagan, spread out over six towns where the Ashiwi have lived for about four thousand years.

The scene plays in my mind as we retrace the Spanish explorer's route in our journey from Gallup, New Mexico, on Highway 602 to the Zuni Pueblo. We note the weathered pickup trucks parked off the highway, but as we drive by we are unable to spot anyone. Since it is October, families must be out among the pinyon pines gathering pine nuts.

Coronado did not find the Seven Cities of Gold, only the isolated villages of the Zuni. Today about ten thousand Zuni live in the largest of the pueblos of New Mexico. The former settlements are clearly demarked by adobe ruins. The homes that we could see today were of simple cinder-block

---

1. Quoted in O'Donnell, "Boundaries of the Sacred."

construction. Isolation from other pueblos of New Mexico made for a distinctive Zuni language and culture. Granted, the physical aspect of the place lacks the romantic appeal of the terraced old adobe buildings of Taos, but if you spend the night at the Inn at Halona or talk with some of the notable artisans, you will soon gain a proper appreciation of Zuni.

For years I have collected stone-carved Zuni animal fetishes and used them in my college lectures on Native American spirituality. I had a vague understanding of their sacred power, but I wanted to visit the source of the fetishes to understand their connection to the sacred.

It turns out that in 1879 there was another spiritual explorer who visited the Zuni Reservation. The U. S. Government had sent Frank Hamilton Cushing with the J. W. Powell Expedition to investigate the mysterious power of the legendary fetishes. Could they be a threat to the United States? Cushing immersed himself in Zuni culture, gained their trust and learned the language. He was initiated into the Bow Priesthood as a War Chief and given the name Medicine Flower. You can read about Cushing's experiences and what he learned about fetishes in his book *Zuni Fetishes*. He encountered an enticing animistic world where, all inanimate objects as well as plant, animals and men, belong to one great system of all conscious and interrelated life. Any element in nature is endowed with a personality analogous to that of the animal whose operations most resemble its manifestations.[2]

For Cushing, the Zuni stone fetishes were sacred living stones.

> It is supposed that the hearts of the great animals of prey are infused with a spirit or medicine of magic influence over the hearts of the animals they prey upon, or the game animals; that their breaths, derived from their hearts, and breathed upon their prey, whether near or far, never fail to overcome them, piercing their hearts and causing their limbs to stiffen, and the animals themselves to lose their strength ... Moreover, these powers, as derived from his heart, are preserved in his fetich, [sic] since his heart still lives, even though his person be changed to stone.[3]

Thus, the Zuni fetish is a vital spiritual aid to (among many things) a successful hunt. But how did the Zuni translate the power of the great animals into the stone fetishes? Kent McManis gives an answer from Zuni mythology.

2. Cushing, *Zuni Fetishes*, 9.
3. Cushing, *Zuni Fetishes*, 15.

Desert Spirit Places

The Zuni believe that the world was once covered with floodwaters, which left it swampy. The Sun Father, revered by the Zuni as the giver of life and light, created twin sons. The Twins realized the world was too wet for humankind to survive and needed to be dried. The Sun Father had given his sons a magic shield, a bow (the rainbow) and arrows (lightning). The Twins placed their shield on the earth, crossed the rainbow and lightning arrows on top of it, and shot an arrow into the point where they crossed. Lightning flew out in each direction creating a tremendous fire. Although this dried the earth, it made it too easy for predators to catch and eat people. So, to save humans, the Twins struck these animals with their lightning, burning and shriveling them into stone. But deep within, the animals' hearts were kept alive, with instructions to help humankind with the magic captured in their hearts. When a Zuni finds a stone that naturally resembles an animal, he believes that it is one of these ancient stone beasts.[4]

Janice, Erik and I stop at the Visitors' Center on the north side Highway 53, halfway through town.

Zuni tribal drummers beat a loud cadence behind me as dancers swirl and stomp, feathers flutter and bells jingle on their costumes. This is the Fall Festival. In front of the Zuni Cultural Center artisans have set up tables to display their work. I approach a woman seated at her table, head bent over in concentration as she delicately works a lump of native turquoise. I want to be respectful and not to ask too many touristy questions. I walk cautiously forward and when my shadow covers her work, she looks up to greet me with a beautiful smile and twinkling eyes.

"Hello. Please sit down."

I am meeting the Zuni fetish artist, Verla Lasiloo-Jim. I do not need to ask a lot of questions because Verla quickly senses my interest and she freely shares her story.

"My husband passed away several years ago. He carved the fetishes. I always watched him at his work and wondered how he decided what animal he would carve. He said he could see the spirit inside the stone and what he was doing was helping the form become what it was meant to be. When he died, it was a tough time and I didn't know what to do. I began to work with his tools and some of the stones that he had left. I began with turtles and frogs. Sometimes what came out was ugly. But I would save it to remind me. There is one over there."

4. McManis, *Zuni Fetishes and Carvings*, 6.

Zuni Pueblo, New Mexico — Zuni Fetish: Living Stones

I could see on the table some very small fetishes, which looked as if they could be placed in a medicine bag as a kind of sacred talisman.

The Spanish invaders and the Christian missionaries tried to stop the practice of fetish-making as it seemed like idolatry.

Verla Lasiloo-Jim had a friend who was a dealer and he began to sell her fetishes and slowly her popularity grew. She is a member of the Mahooty, Lasiloo and Laiwakete interrelated family clan, known for their use of a variety of materials such as stone, wood and shells in making fetishes.

The drumming is growing louder and I must draw closer to Ms. Lasiloo-Jim, as she has a soft voice.

"Are all the fetishes sacred?" I ask.

"If the medicine man blesses them, they should be used in the traditional manner. They need to be cared for by feeding them with blue corn meal. Some people keep them in turquoise-encrusted pots."

"Are they alive?"

"I can tell you that if I am bothered by a problem or worry, I can pray over a fetish and the answer to my concern will be given to me." She seems to be inviting me to stay as long as I wish, as she continues to work on the turquoise.

"What will it become?"

"I don't know yet, but I think it is a bear."

I purchase a fetish. As I leave to join my family she says, "Here is my card with my address. Let me know if you want me to make something for you. You can even send me a drawing or a photo. I see your black poodle over there. I can make a poodle for you. Please let me know."

A few days later we are at a gift shop at Grand Canyon National Park where an array of Zuni fetishes are comfortably sheltering in a glass case. I see a stone bear with a turquoise line running from its mouth to the heart. Kent McManis speaks about this specifically:

> An inlaid, carved, or painted "heartline" represents the breath path leading to the magical power in the fetish's heart... A bundle consisting of various stones, shells, and/or arrowheads is sometimes tied onto a fetish. The bundle serves as an offering that empowers the fetish to better aid the user.[5]

All very well, but with the variety available, exactly how does one go about choosing a fetish? McManis says that he has a simple rule for fetish

---

5. McManis, *Zuni Fetishes and Carvings*, 10.

selection; if the fetish talks to him, he will buy it no matter what the animal is or who carved it. "I believe that fetishes usually pick you out."[6]

Now I am at Richardson's Trading Post on Route 66 in downtown Gallup, New Mexico. In my hand is a turquoise bear fetish, which has somehow caught my attention. The red heartline runs from nose to heart. Was it calling to me specifically? Am I simply taken by a quaint relic from a "primitive" culture? What is going on here? As anyone with an academic degree in the Western world, I have been schooled in the mindset of the Enlightenment, and I feel dissonance. Am I betraying all I know? I trace the bear's heartline with a hesitant finger. With regard to this odd discomfiting, the Canadian philosopher Charles Taylor comes to mind. He summarizes some helpful insights in his book *A Secular Age*:

> Almost everyone can agree that one of the big differences between us and our ancestors of five hundred years ago is that they lived in an "enchanted" world, and we do not; at the very least, we live in a much less "enchanted" world. We might think of this as our having "lost" a number of beliefs and the practices which they made possible. But more, the enchanted world was one in which these forces could cross a porous boundary and shape our lives, psychic and physical. One of the big differences between us and them is that we live with a much firmer sense of the boundary between self and other. We are "buffered" selves. We have changed.[7]

Like the world of my European ancestors five hundred years ago, the Zuni world today is a porous world, aware of demons, witches and dark forces that can threaten, and at the same time be open to ecstatic and mystical experiences with the Creator. We "modern" folk with our buffered selves are closed off to both kinds of powers

Yet in many people there continues to be a fascination, a longing, a restlessness that brings spiritual seekers like me to Zuni and Verla Lasaloo-Jim.

Johnathan Napier describes the divide between the spiritual and the secular in Charles Taylor's work and how this division is immaterial to Native American world views.

> ... Taylor introduces his "immanent frame," which describes how people understand their relation to the supernatural. People either live in interaction with the supernatural or live separate from it.

---

6. McManis, *Zuni Fetishes and Carvings*, 139.
7. Taylor, "Buffered and Porous Selves."

Taylor depicts this as a divide between the porous and the buffered self. The porous self has an enchanted worldview; it sees itself as interacting with the spiritual world; it is vulnerable and open to forces beyond the physical realm.[8]

Sacred power is found both in objects such as the Zuni fetish and in places. In the Western world, accompanying the Enlightenment, science and a focus on human reason, a process of disenchantment set in, as the buffered self dismissed or compartmentalized spiritual experiences. Initiated by the philosophy of René Descartes, this modern sort of self turns radically inward, becoming personal and private. Indigenous cultures such as the Zuni, in contrast, turn outward—to nature, the land and communal relationships. There is no separation between the material world and the spiritual realm; all is infused with the sacred. While the Western world compartmentalizes, the Zuni seek harmony and balance in a unified world.

As I hold the bear fetish in my hand, a soft-spoken and patient Navajo saleswoman speaks to me across the glass display case about the fetish. A porous soul speaks to a buffered soul about the sacred:

"The bear is the best mediator with the Creator because it has the closest resemblance to humans. The bear has power, strength and intelligence to help you. The bear can help you make peace in times of conflict and guide you when you have spiritual challenges."

I purchase the bear fetish and she wraps it carefully in cotton and places it in a protective box. She smiles as she hands me a transparent plastic bag with the fetish and a tiny Ziploc bag filled with what looks like blue cornmeal.

I am back at home. I am holding the bear fetish, which I keep in a glass case above the ritual artifacts of the Day of the Dead that I have collected over the years. The fetish is warm in my hand. It is not one of the sacred fetishes blessed by the Zuni priest, who would have animated the figure with a real spirit presence.

I trace with my thumb the red lifeline running from the bear's mouth to its heart. The artist who created this believed in "the Spirit that lives in all things." The bear fetish would be a messenger and protector from that Spirit. As I hold the bear, a single word comes to my mind—kinship. The Zuni believe that all created things, animate and inanimate, are connected. There are similar words from St. Paul in my Christian tradition:

---

8. Napier, "Interfaith Dialogue Theory," 83–84.

> In Him all things in heaven and on earth were created, things visible and invisible, whether thrones or dominions or rulers or powers - all things have been created through him and for him. He is before all things, and in him all things hold together.[9]

At the heart of the spirituality of St. Ignatius Loyola is the belief that we encounter God in all things. Our spirituality and awareness of the presence of God grows deeper as we draw closer to our kindship with all created things.

And now I am remembering words of the Trappist monk Thomas Merton:

> It is good and praiseworthy to look at some real created thing and feel and appreciate its reality. Just let the reality of what is real sink into you . . . for through real things we can reach Him who is infinitely real.[10]

In my study of world religions it is readily apparent that most traditions create sacred images. Most of these have been animated by blessings from a priest or shaman. While they may be sacred and fed, like this bear fetish, a statue of Shiva in a Hindu temple, or a statue of Quan Yin in a Taoist temple, they are tangible means to connect with the Divine.

---

9. Colossians 1:16–17
10. Merton, *School of Charity*, 61.

Zuni Pueblo, New Mexico — Zuni Fetish: Living Stones

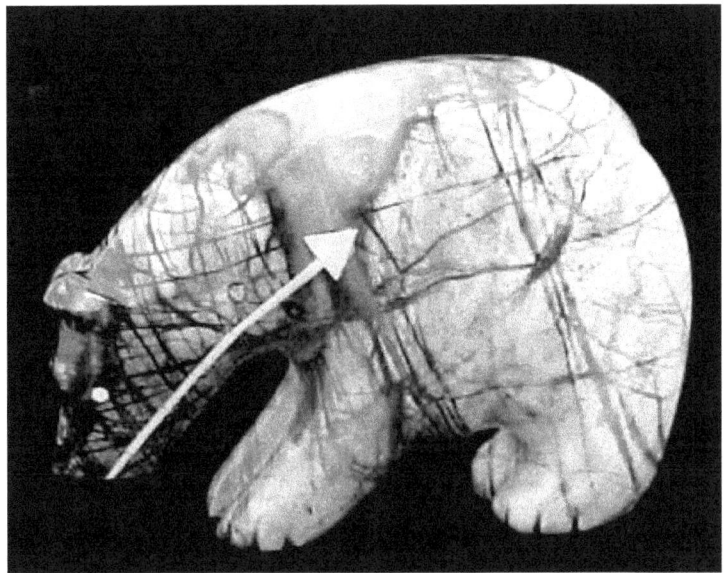

Traditional Zuni Bear Fetish. 2009. Photo by Techninjas.

The Zuni may pray to the bear fetish for courage as he meets a particular challenge. I may kneel in church and pray to Our Lady of Guadalupe. They are not the same, but they are similar connections to the Sacred.

The buffered self, fostered by science and Enlightenment philosophy, has distanced us from our kinship with the natural world.

John Swanson observes:

> In modern society, animals have lost their central role in cultural organization. When animals are no longer viewed as guiding spirits nor connected to us by sacred rituals that guide our behavior, animals lose their significance retaining only their function as secular emblems. Vestiges of these connects between animals and societal groupings remain in the naming of our sports teams and lodges: The Miami Dolphins, Detroit Tigers, and Chicago Bulls; in the Lions Club and Elks Lodge, and in the stuffed animals we buy for our children. Revered spirit animals are reduced to team mascots.[11]

I am grateful for solitary sunset walks into desert spirit places, renewing my kinship with all created things.

---

11. Swanson, *Communing with Nature*, 107.

6.

Abiquiu, New Mexico
—Passionate Christians

What can we gain by sailing to the moon if we are not able to cross the abyss that separates us from ourselves? This is the most important of all voyages of discovery, and without it all the rest are not only useless but disastrous.

—Thomas Merton [1]

THE EAST GERMAN BORDER guard held my passport photo up beside my face and sighed a deep sigh, which he followed by a long silence. Suddenly, he shouted something at me in German. I am fluent in German but at that moment I was having a brain freeze. He shouted the same phrase at me twice more and the guard on his right bristled to attention. I looked at her inquiringly. She responded in a soft voice, "He wants to know where you are going today."

"I have a hotel reservation in Magdeburg. Here are my reservation papers."

She quickly looked over the papers and returned them to me with the passport. "Thank you. Have a nice visit to the German Democratic Republic."

Bad cop, good cop.

Heart pounding and with parched mouth, I drove the rented Mitsubishi Colt past the grim concrete towers. I could see several guards eyeing me

---

1. Merton, *Wisdom of the Desert*, 11.

as I left the checkpoint at Helmstedt, heading east on the autobahn toward Magdeburg.

The year is 1980. I am on a two-week study trip in Germany doing research for a magazine article contrasting the vitality of Christian spirituality in West Germany and East Germany. I had already visited Braunschweig, West Germany, fifty miles west of Helmstedt, to interview seminary professors and pastors about West German spirituality.

An Evangelical Lutheran seminary professor had reported, "My experience has been that many of our students who study for ministry had as a first choice for profession to be a lawyer or university professor. But failing the entrance requirements they chose the ministry as their backup plan. It is not a bad choice. The State gives financial support to the Church through taxes. The work is not difficult and if you like to read and study, this is the place to be."

In West Germany, there seemed to be none of the anxiety about fundraising or parish conflict that American pastors know so well. But West German state support of religion, directly or indirectly, resulted in active participation of less than 3 percent of the population.

What would I find as I headed towards Magdeburg, into the depths of Cold War Soviet-occupied territory?

The first sign of the city is a massive pile of ancient stones faintly visible in the distance: the Magdeburg Cathedral. My hotel, The Internationale, was nearby. After checking in, I walked through the old town toward the majestic Elba River. Barges laden with coal and lumber pushed upstream, perhaps going to Dresden.

I walked towards a church which was a block away to my left. A surprise. Gathered outside was a group of university students. I introduced myself as a college professor from California, necessarily keeping the parish-priest identity under wraps. Then I saw a stocky, older man approaching. After introductions and with my identity as a professor established, Pastor Georg Nuglish invited me into the assembly. In a large hall, several tables were pulled together to create an inclusive square of seated participants. I could see that there were over one hundred in attendance. How strange! These young people had lived their whole lives under the atheist theology of Communism, yet here they were, so many of them, at a church event. Pastor Georg told me before the meeting that this was the largest college-age religious group in the German Democratic Republic, (DDR).

The presenter that night was a Roman Catholic priest from Karl Marx Stadt, whose topic was "The Socialist themes in the Gospel of Mark." He told me, "We meet every Wednesday for discussion of theology and philosophy. The students really want to be here and it is not without risk. Participation here can compromise their advancement at the university."

"So, you have to be careful about your discussion topics?" I asked.

"Yes, of course. I know there are Stasi agents or informers here. The philosophers we choose to discuss are on the margins. We do push the envelope. But I want to help the students to be critical thinkers. That will not happen in their university experience."

After the presentation and discussion of the evening topic. Pastor Georg introduced me: California! Exotic.

Students gazed at me with hard focus and the questions flew like barbs. Why do Americans abuse black people? Why is there so much racism in your country? Why do Americans insist on polluting the world? My responses did not seem to be adequate.

As the meeting closed, all were invited downstairs to the *bierkeller*. Now this was amazing —a college-age church group with their own bar downstairs! I went with the group and shared the beer. That was when the real questions were asked. What is life like in California? Had I met the Beach Boys? Do they still have cowboys? Had I ever seen a movie star? It was a wonderful ending to the tensions of the discussion group.

The next day I invited Pastor George and his wife Ulla for an outing. We drove to the medieval town of Tangermünde, which still had the ancient city walls and six-hundred year-old *fachtwerk* houses.

Pastor George and Ulla shared with me what life was like for them in the DDR.

"Being a pastor here is a precarious profession. The family suffers. When Ulla was in the hospital last year, they put her in an isolation ward to limit access to her. Our daughter graduated at the top of her high school this year, but she can't go to the best university, because her father is a pastor."

"What could happen to you if you cross the line? Would you go to prison?"

"That is unlikely. Probably they would kick me and my family out of the DDR as corrupting influences. The ones I really worry about are the students. They have a passion for our religious studies. They begin to question life as it is and if they become too critical, there could be real trouble for them. Some students have disappeared. Maybe they are in the prison at Bautzen."

On Sunday, I attended the *Gottesdienst* at the church. The service was much like the Lutheran liturgies in which I had participated in the West—except the building was packed. One reason was that the city had been severely damaged in World War II bombing; few churches had been rebuilt. But there was wonderful energy in the singing and presence of the parishioners. Was spirituality stronger in Communist East Germany? There was certainly a cost to discipleship, as Dietrich Bonhoeffer declared.

My observations about State support of religion and the dilution of spiritual passion in West Germany contrasted with the fervor and spiritual-seeking that I witnessed among East German students. I am reminded of an earlier time of State support for Christianity.

When the Roman Emperor Constantine gave Imperial endorsement to Christianity after decades of violent persecution of Christians, great church buildings and basilicas were constructed. The underground, secret house churches were no longer necessary. Christianity could grow and thrive openly in this new world of official sanction.

Comfortable, established religion does seem to stimulate a counter-point of intense, passionate spirituality which (necessarily) retreats into the wilderness. We find a Western Church example in St. Benedict of Nursia.

Benedict (c. 500 CE) grew up in a Roman noble family—a good start in the world for any young man. But something pulled him away from his friends, schooling and love-life and away from the city. He hated the life of the city, its moral duplicity, the compromises it forced on him. He left Rome for a place forty miles into the Simbruini mountains, the village of Enfide.

A precarious, narrow path climbed the steep side of the mountains to a cave, ten feet deep and five hundred feet above the sky-blue waters of a lake. Higher up the slope was the monastery home of the monk Romanus. Romanus responded to Benedict's restless search for an authentic life with God, gave him the monk's habit of his community and encouraged him to live as a hermit in the cave above the lake. Many curious stories about Benedict emanate from this time, not least:

> One day, the Devil brought before his imagination a beautiful woman he had formerly known, inflaming his heart with strong desire for her. Immediately, Benedict stripped off his clothes

and rolled into a thorn-bush until his body was lacerated. Thus, through the wounds of the body, he cured the wounds of his soul.[2]

In these three years as a hermit, Benedict came to know his True Self and grew in communion with God. When the old abbot of the monastery above the hermitage died, the monks were attracted to Benedict's radiant presence. He brought his wisdom about life with God to the monks. Nonetheless, the malevolent among them tried to poison him. Benedict retreated to his cave. His enemies continued to try to kill him or seduce him with temptations. To escape these assaults, Benedict left the area and eventually established, through his integrity and charisma, twelve other monasteries. In 530 CE he founded the great monastery at Monte Casino which still exists today.

Monasteries, like churches, can become too comfortable and drift from the challenges of the teachings of Jesus in the Gospels. The danger of degeneration is addressed throughout the work for which Benedict is best known, his Rule, used today by Roman Catholic and Anglican monastics throughout the world. How do you sustain a religious community made up with flawed, self-centered humans who can be in constant conflict? The Rule, in succinct, pointed paragraphs, is a practical guide to how to live a Christ-centered life here in this world, and how to efficiently run a monastery. When I read the Rule, I can see how a monastic community is like a family, and one could boil down this guidance to even a small family. You keep the wandering minds of monks busy and focused on God in two ways: Ora et Labora—Prayer and Work. So, Benedict divided the day into scheduled prayer services which focused on the Psalms in the Bible. There would be eight hours of prayer, eight hours of sleep and eight hours of work in the fields, in the library or in the community serving others. If you visit any Western Christian monastery today, you will experience this same schedule still lived out faithfully.

But just as Benedict had found in his youth, there were others who felt that community life compromised the demands of life with God. The answer for them would be found in the desert.

Pachomius grew up in a pagan Egyptian family. At the age of twenty-one he was conscripted into the Roman army. He was in effect a slave recruit and kept in confinement at night. He encountered Christians who visited him and others in prison and brought food and clothing. After several visits from the Christians, he asked, "Why do you do this?"

2. Pirlo, *My First Book of Saints*, 145–47.

ABIQUIU, NEW MEXICO—PASSIONATE CHRISTIANS

"We are Christians. This is what our Lord commanded us to do."

"Tell me what it means to be a Christian."—The door to faith was opened to Pachomius. He was able to escape from the army, joined the Christians and was baptized in the year 314. Passionate Christians at this time were leaving the cities of Egypt, Palestine and Syria and heading out into the desert for solitude and silence, to be closer to God. It was in the desert that Pachomius met Anthony of Egypt.

Male and female Christian hermits sought isolated *wadis*, (arroyos, or dry-washes) where they dug small caves into the embankments and lived off the land. Solitude and silence were preferred. Occasionally, they would gather for a worship event. These Desert Fathers and Mothers sought a life stripped of the accoutrements of civilization, which would lead to the true self, the Christ-self. They wanted to be freed from the false self—that is: who I am, what I have, what I do, and what others think of me. Much of the collected wisdom of these desert sages would become for generations of seekers, practical guidance for the journey to the true self and away from the temptations of the false self.

As the Christ-self developed in him, Pachomius believed that God told him to build shelters where the monks could live together. He built his first monastery in about the year 320 at Tabennisi, Egypt. Soon his brother John, and a hundred other monks had gathered there and Pachomius organized them into a formal unit. The Rule he developed as Abba, or Abbot, became foundational for the Eastern Orthodox Church. This Rule came to anchor the life of Eastern monks' life with God and together in community. But it may be said that here community life is not the emphasis; at the heart of Pachomius' desert spirituality was discernment centered in the individual's intimate relationship with God. Ultimately, as St. Anthony of Egypt counseled, a man or a woman stood alone before God: "Therefore, whatever you see your soul to desire according to God, do that thing, and you shall keep your heart safe" (*Verba* no. 1).

The American Trappist, Thomas Merton, studied the wisdom of these desert fathers and mothers, he saw the hard work of detaching the true self from ego.

He could not retain the slightest identification with his superficial, transient, self-constructed self. He had to lose himself in the inner, hidden reality of a self that was transcendent, mysterious, half-known, and lost in Christ.[3]

The wisdom of the ancient desert fathers and mothers still guides us today. There is a raw simplicity that comes from their personal experience of wrestling with the false self and seeing their true selves emerging from the practice of silence, solitude and prayer. Their sayings were passed on in an oral tradition and endure today because they give practical guidance in how to love God and our neighbor. Here is an example from this tradition:

> They said of Abbot Pambo that in the very hour when he departed this life he said to the holy men who stood by him: From the time, I came to this place in the desert, and built me a cell, and dwelt here, I do not remember eating bread that was not earned by the work of my own hands, nor do I remember saying anything for which I was sorry even until this hour. And thus, I go to the Lord as one who has not even made a beginning in the service of God.[4]

Thomas Merton, one of the most influential spiritual writers of the twentieth century, had his own desert monastic experience at the Monastery of Christ in the Desert, near Santa Fe, New Mexico.

The Jemez Mountain and Sangre De Cristo ranges frame Santa Fe, enclosing a powerful desert spirit place. For over a thousand years, Pueblo Indians have encountered the sacred here both in their traditional spirituality and more recently in Spanish Catholicism. After eastern religions were brought into America on a large scale in the 1960s and 1970s, Santa Fe has become a center point for world spiritualities, including Sikhism and Tibetan Buddhism. I wonder what it is about Santa Fe that has made it so fertile for spiritual exploration? My experience has been that recent residents have come here as spiritual seekers. Many seem to be people of means and college-educated. It is a sophisticated population, including artists and writers. It is not surprising, therefore, that Thomas Merton came to the monastery at Abiquiu in 1968.

He had joined the Trappist Community of Gethsemane, Kentucky in the mid-1940s. He chose one of the most severe Cistercian monasteries, where silence was the rule, food and housing were spartan, and the monks worked hard at manual labor. In this vestige of medieval Christianity, Merton found freedom and creativity. His famous book *The Seven Storey Mountain*, is his autobiography. He didn't want to write it, but the Abbot,

---

3. Merton, *Wisdom of the Desert*, 7.
4. Merton, *Wisdom of the Desert*, 26.

discerning the creative writing talent cooking within Merton, ordered him to write it. It was to become one of the best-selling books on spirituality.

Rather than letting the silence and solitude foster a withdrawal from the world, Merton found that these elements drew him deep into communion with God, whose inspiration ignited in Merton more passionate writing about struggles in the outer world for civil rights and nuclear disarmament. As a mystic, he found partnership in world spiritualities other than Christianity. He became a serious student of Chinese philosophy and Zen Buddhism, and developed deep friendships with spiritual leaders, including the Dalai Lama. For several years I have used the film *Merton: A Film Biography*, to help my world religions students at Saddleback College see how an orthodox Roman Catholic monk could become a strong bridge between world religions.

By the 1960s, Merton received a rare gift: permission from the abbot to live as a hermit, living in a forest hut by himself away from communal life in the monastery. Here silence and solitude enriched his long hours in prayer and meditation. In his reading in Scripture and the Desert Fathers the image of the desert became an inviting companion to silence and solitude.

In his book *Thoughts in Solitude*, he contemplates:

> The desert Fathers believed that the wilderness had been created as supremely valuable in the eyes of God precisely because it had no value to men. The wasteland was the land that could never be wasted by men because it offered them nothing. There was nothing to attract them. There was nothing to exploit.[5]

Many writers and fellow seekers have commented on this theme of Merton's dynamic and resonant spirituality. For example, Robert Daggy writes:

The mountain may be the most pervasive image in Merton's journey metaphors, but the desert—-mysterious, deceptively barren, frequently foreboding—was a special and holy place for him. The desert theme resonates through his life and work—from the images in his poetry to those in his journals. There was, of course, his book *The Wisdom of the Desert*

---

5. Merton, *Thoughts in Solitude*, 5.

(1960) in which he "rendered" several of the stories of the Desert Fathers of the fourth century.[6]

The problem with being a famous writer and monk meant for Merton a constant flow of friends and visitors. He received permission from the Abbot at Gethsemane to explore another place for his hermitage. And that is how he came to the Benedictine monastery of Christ in the Desert at Abiquiu, New Mexico.

You really have to want to come to this raw desert wilderness within the Chama River Canyon, seventy-five miles north of Santa Fe. Driving past the home of the great painter, Georgia O'Keefe, and the Ghost Ranch Center, you turn onto Forest Road 151, which is thirteen miles of rough dirt road off US 84. You drive through a sagebrush ocean walled in by looming rusty red cliffs. It is a breathtaking drive as the road climbs hundreds of feet above the Chama River. This is a Class 1 good dirt road, but when it rains, the road has the consistency of pancake-batter and is impassable.

At the end of the Forest Road 151 is the "mystical nowhere" that Merton sought: Christ in the Desert Monastery. Here is how he himself describes the scene:

> The monastic church, designed by the Japanese architect George Nakashima, fits perfectly into its setting. Stark, lonely, stately in its simplicity, it gazes out over the sparse irrigated fields into the widening valley. The tower is like a watchman looking for something or someone of whom it does not speak. The architectural masterpiece is a perfect expression, in adobe brick and plaster, of the monastic spirit.[7]

For myself, I find that when I go on retreat it takes at least one day to mentally shake off the journey and detox from the daily stimuli that caffeinate my restless life. But here the struggle is somewhat less tumultuous than usual. The dry, sweet silence and solitude, along with breathtaking beauty can be felt and seen from every angle. The desert spirit seeps into the body and I am enfolded in its precious embrace. Every few hours, there is a chapel service with the monks, based on the 1500-year-old schedule set up by St. Benedict in his Rule. *Ora et labora:* The routine, the rhythm of work and prayer builds a healthy monastic community. The monks chant several psalms at each service, sung antiphonally: the monks on one side of the oratory sing, then the other side answers, in a hypnotic rhythm. I listen to the

6. Daggy, *Thomas Merton.*
7. Merton, *Monastery of Christ in the Desert.*

readings from the Bible and the Voice of God speaks to me in the here and now of my life.

Christ in the Desert Monastery. 2003. Photo by Jeffrey Zoeller.

Merton arrived at Christ in the Desert, searching for a mystical nowhere. In the desert, he found communion with the people of the Exodus, totally dependent on God's grace for daily survival, and with Jesus, whose temptations revealed to him his true self as God's beloved. This desert spirit place revived him as he considered what was ahead for him personally, and for his monastic community in Kentucky:

> In our monasticism, we have been content to find our way to a kind of peace, a simple undisturbed thoughtful life, and this is certainly good, but is it good enough? I, for one, realize that now I need more. Not simply to be quiet, somewhat productive, to pray, to read, to cultivate leisure, live in peace, let change come quietly and invisibly on the inside . . . A return to genuine practice, right effort, need to push on to the great doubt. Need for the Spirit. Hang on to the clear light![8]

After his last visit to Christ in the Desert, Merton traveled to San Francisco, where he was hosted by his old friend and poet Lawrence Ferlinghetti. Merton was on his way to Bangkok, Thailand, for a conference for

8. Merton, *Woods, Shore, Desert*, 48.

Christian and non-Christian monks. At the time the communist authorities of Southeast Asia were making a great effort to bring their significant populations of Buddhist monks under control. Merton made a presentation in which he contrasted Marxism and monasticism, contending that the philosophy of the common life doesn't work with Marxism; it does work within monasticism. At the afternoon break, Merton took a shower to cool off from the humid weather. His body was discovered a brief time later. There has been a mystery about his death. Did someone not approve of his criticism of communism? Did someone not approve of his criticism of American involvement in the war in Vietnam? The consensus today is that his body was found close to an electric fan. He must have touched the ungrounded fan with his wet hands and was electrocuted. Ironically, his remains returned to America in a US Air Force plane along with remains of American soldiers killed in the war that he had spoken against. Thomas Merton was buried at his Gethsemane Abbey home in Kentucky, perhaps the best-known monk of all time, certainly of his time.

The monastery of Christ in the Desert extends traditional Benedictine hospitality to visitors seeking that mystical Nowhere. Men and women can stay in one of eleven rooms in the guest house for private retreats and join the monks for worship and meals. The minimum stay is two nights. You may help with *labora*—manual labor with the monks, which may include work in the monastery garden. The rooms are comfortable but there is no electricity in the guest houses and no cell-phone nor Internet service. The water comes from the monastery well. The church bell signals meal times and prayer times. The monks make their own brew from hops grown in the garden and the beer is sold at the upscale grocery chain, Whole Foods Market.

Walking around the property at Abiquiu reminds me very much of Mt. Calvary Episcopal Monastery that once sat high in the hills above Montecito, California, before it was destroyed in a fire a few years ago. I made many retreats there over the past fifty years. Both establishments have extensive desert plantings and both have walks down to a river. Christ in the Desert has trails leading to the Chama River, which runs all year.

The Chapel is rich in iconography. There are large icons of St. John the Baptist, the ultimate Desert Saint, and St. Benedict. The Blessed Sacrament is closeted within a montage of icons. Behind the altar are huge windows which give views of the vaulting cliffs which are the protective backdrop to the monastery.

The monks at Christ in the Desert want you to know that you are invited to visit and make retreat at this special desert spirit place.

7.

Orange Park Acres, Southern California —Leaving The House of Prayer

> However, (Thomas Merton said), the usual road to contemplation is through the desert, a barren land with no trees, beauty or water. This prospect is so frightening that we are afraid to enter. In that desert God is nowhere to be found. Yet some people sense that peace is to be found in the heart of darkness, so they keep still, they stop trying to force prayer and meditation and other spiritual exercises, and they patiently trust in God. In the midst of darkness and emptiness, God leads them to the promised land.
>
> —William O. Paulsell,[1]

A HEAVY FEELING HIT the pit of my stomach as I walked through the portal into the House of Prayer for the last time. Another June heatwave had descended over southern California and these dry foothills of Orange Park Acres, but the desert plants surrounding the complex of Santa Fe-style adobe casitas are radiant and surging with life. To my left is a thirty-foot agave century plant in all its glory, the thick green stem topped with a huge vanilla-colored flower. Soon it will collapse into itself and wither. Yet I can see baby agaves already emerging around the mother plant. This is indeed a fertile place for desert plants—and desert souls.

I have come to my last spiritual direction session with Father Gordon Moreland SJ, before he departs to a new pastoral assignment. I first came to this priests' retreat center for the Roman Catholic Diocese of Orange in 1992, five years after Father Gordon arrived and only six years after our son

---

1. Paulsell, *Rules for Prayer*, 135.

Erik's catastrophic health crisis. I have had twenty-five years of spiritual nourishment here. A serious investment.

I pace about the desert garden planted along the walkway that leads to the retreatant rooms and the chapel. I take photographs to help me remember this place that has become so important to me—it would be terrible for it to fade from my mind.

Father Gordon greets me as I enter his office. I sit in a chair facing him and the windows behind him frame the abundant agave and cactus outside. We often shared information about growing and caring for desert plants. Too much water will kill them. I have sat in this old chair, once a month, for all these years, across from Gordon and the desert outside. This has been my sacred place. From here I have negotiated interior spiritual deserts.

Walter Bruggemann writes:

> Place is space which has historical meanings, where some things have happened which are now remembered and which provide continuity and identity across generations. Place is space in which important words have been spoken which have established identity, defined vocation and envisioned destiny. Place is space in which vows have been exchanged, promises have been made, and demands have been issued.[2]

As I look about Gordon's office—a last opportunity to to fix my impressions, my gaze rests on a large portrait of St. Ignatius Loyola, the sixteenth-century Spanish soldier who founded the Jesuit order. Behind me hangs a Chinese poem in beautiful calligraphy, flanked by two Chinese figurines. Father Gordon has visited China every autumn over the last few years, connecting with his Jesuit missionary roots. Then my eye catches something through the window behind him: a coyote dashing through the garden.

---

2. Brueggemann, *Land*, 5.

Entrance to House of Prayer Retreat Center, Orange, California. 2016. Photo by author.

    I find myself reminiscing about my life before coming to the House of Prayer. In 1990, after Janice and I returned from Massachusetts General Hospital, where for a month Erik had been fighting the raging brain fever of encephalitis, I visited Sister Jeanne Fallon of the Sisters of Saint Joseph of Orange at their Spirituality Center. My initial motivation was to find help in dealing with the aftermath of Erik's return home and our embarking on the difficult daily routine of care for a severely disabled child. But there was something else: deeper down, it was my life of secrets that compelled me to seek Sister Jeanne's counsel. As I look back, this was a grace of God that was compelling me.

    Sister Jeanne saw the inner turmoil gnawing at me and urged me to begin the Spiritual Exercises of Saint Ignatius with her. For one year we met weekly. I followed this five-hundred-year-old curriculum of daily contemplation of a Bible passage, leading me through the events of the life of Jesus and his Resurrection. We focused on becoming more aware of God's presence and the movements of grace in my life.

    At that point I had gone through theological training, all sorts of spiritual practice, and more than fifteen years of ministry as an Episcopal priest, taking seriously the spiritual welfare of two thriving parishes, so you would think I would have my own spiritual life moving along at a good pace. However, it is not too much to admit that in these weekly sessions with Sister Jeanne, I came to know Jesus for the first time. Oh, I was pretty familiar with the Scriptures: they were the ancient hallowed texts on which I preached at every Sunday Mass. But now in my contemplation, the holy words seemed as if they had been written just that morning.

Sister Jeanne had warned me that the Spiritual Exercises constituted a deeply interior process rather than a therapeutic overlay or some sort of program for sedating me against the stresses of life. She also warned me that with God there are no secrets and now I was being invited to be real and honest with God.

In this context, my addicted life opened up to the light: how I had been using credit cards to pay for family needs, personal pleasures and parish projects. I owed about twelve thousand dollars at that point and my wife did not know about it. Yes, I could have rationalized that eventually I would pay off the bill and that our tight income necessitated this overspending. But I was barely able to make minimum payments and I was hiding this from Janice. I told Sister Jeanne about my fear of being discovered. Finally, one day I resolved to tell Janice about the debt. I thought the world was going to end. But it didn't. Janice is nothing if not immensely practical. She had experience with Al-Anon, and urged me to go to an addiction recovery group. That same night I went to an open Alcoholics Anonymous meeting in Dana Point.

I was on a spiritual high: The Secret was out! When I came to the door at the AA meeting, greeters were there to welcome me and there was joy in that place. New Life. In the meeting, three people in recovery shared how they decided to come to AA. The surprise of the evening was the testimony of one of my philosophy students at Saddleback Community College. He shared how his life had collapsed. He had been at the verge of suicide because of his long-time addiction to alcohol. But something led him to his first AA meeting and his life changed. This was like hearing the best sermon on Easter Day.

I began to attend Saturday morning meetings of Adult Children of Alcoholics at the psychiatric facility in San Juan Capistrano. There I learned that my compulsive spending and secrets were common to many people coming out of an alcoholic family. I also learned that the antidote to secrecy is honesty, which led to the fundamental realization that my life had become so disordered as to be unmanageable. And I learned that the grace of God and my working a program of honesty and transparency would lead me through each day.

Ron Rolheiser writes:

> Sobriety is ultimately not about alcohol or some drug. It's about honesty and transparency. And, like honesty and transparency, it is not all or nothing, but has degrees. We are all sober, more or less, according to the degree that our lives are an open book with nothing hidden in the closet.[3]

To which he adds:

> To live in the light means to live in honesty, pure and simple, to be transparent, to not have part of us hidden as a dark secret.
>
> All conversion and recovery programs worthy of the name are based on bringing us to this type of honesty. We move toward spiritual health precisely by flushing out our sickest secrets and bringing them into the light. It's the hiding of something, the lying, the dishonesty, the deception, the resentment we harbor toward those who stand between us and our addiction, that does the real damage to us and to those we love.[4]

It was Sister Jeanne who sent me to Father Gordon to continue spiritual direction. He is a revered retreat leader and spiritual director, not a therapist. He brought me back to the practice of some of the essentials of the Spiritual Exercises, reminding me of God's deep love for me and the invitation to friendship with Jesus. I practiced the Examen of Conscience each night before sleep. It is five-part prayer which goes something like this:

Presence: I invite God's presence and help.

Gratitude: I recall two or three things that happened in the day for which I am grateful. I savor them and thank God.

Review: I review the day from beginning to end. I notice where I sensed God's presence. I try to remember everything—from large to small. When did I feel and give love, joy, hope and peace?

Sorrow: I may have some regrets about today and offenses I may have committed and ask for God's forgiveness.

Grace: I ask for God's grace for the next day.

3. Rolheiser, *"Honesty as Sobriety."*
4. Rolheiser, "To Live in the Light."

Orange Park Acres, Southern California

As I prayed this Daily Examen, it helped me to see my entire day as an ongoing prayer. I could look back to see and remember where God was with me and be grateful.

I walked through many of life's deserts with Father Gordon and Jesus. During those first ten years of my coming to the House of Prayer, we did not know whether Erik would live much longer; they were years of countless ER visits and hospitalizations. Life at my parish was sometimes messy with conflicts with my bishop, parishioners or staff. I had several opportunities to move up the ladder to a larger parish or to become a bishop myself. Through all of this, Father Gordon helped me to follow the simple and sensible tools for discernment of the Spiritual Exercises: how to make the decision to which God is guiding me, the spirits of light and darkness pulling in opposite directions. I always seemed to forget too easily the grace whereby God brought my family, my parish or myself through a crisis. I could rejoice briefly in amazing grace and then, as soon as a new crisis or challenge arose I would forget. If there is one gift Father Gordon gave me that I most treasure, it is his ability to help me remember again those graces that have brought me home.

I am sitting in the study of my spiritual director; the desert light streaming through the window touches the portrait of Saint Ignatius. I contemplate how the remembrance of unexpected, astonishing graces and this place, the House of Prayer, are connected. As I prepare to leave, the feelings of longing and displacement were strong, because of the gift of Father Gordon's friendship.

Memory is embedded in a place, this House of Prayer. The memory is more than my personal story. There is also the narrative flow of all those who have received spiritual direction, who have stayed here for retreats, who have participated in support groups and the daily Mass in the chapel.

> Each person effectively reshaped [this place] by making his story a thread in the meaning of this place, and also has to come to terms with the many layers of story that already exists here (at this House of Prayer).[5]

I will remember all that God has done for me through these years at the House of Prayer. While I will continue to visit Father Gordon for spiritual direction at his new location, I leave this House of Prayer grateful

---

5. Sheldrake, *Spaces for the Sacred*, 16.

for the peace, joy and hope that I have found here. I leave some of my own spirit here as a blessing for those yet to come.

8.

Three Mesas: Hopi, Arizona—Sacred Masks

> The sale of a sacred object cannot be dismissed with the wave of a hand as a mere commercial transaction.
> —Philip Breeden, U.S. embassy, Paris[1]

THE ANCIENT, CARVED COTTONWOOD mask, decorated with eagle feathers and earth-pigment paints stares blankly at an observer from a shelf in a Paris auction house. The display counter is cluttered with Hopi pottery, kachina figures and sacred altar decorations once hidden in the protective darkness of a kiva—the room used by Puebloans for ritual.

As I studied the photograph in the *New York Times* article, I imagined other sacred objects that could be on another shelf: perhaps a silver pyx containing hosts of the blessed body of Christ; or a treasured Torah scroll from Jerusalem; a hand-copied Qu'ran from Kufa, Iraq; a revered scroll of the Rig Veda from India; and a Tibetan Buddhist Sutra from a monastery high in the Himalayas. I imagine all of these for sale in the same auction house. And I wonder how Muslims, Jews, Christians, Buddhists and Hindus would react if they read about a public auction of these sacred articles? It is not difficult to suppose there would be a vast international reaction, generated by social media, condemning such a sale, indignant CNN commentaries, angry crowds beating down the doors of that Paris auction house.

Reacting to the outcry of another auction of Hopi sacred masks, the auction house EVE contends: "No American law has been violated. There has been no illegal operation." The masks were the property of a French collector who lived in the USA for thirty years.

1. Quoted in Mashberg, "Despite Legal Challenges."

But though the United States considers many tribal entities to be separate nations, the French government does not recognize the Hopi as part of the international community. Jewish families, whose relatives died in the Holocaust, who challenge French courts over ownership of valuable art stolen by the Nazis, have had similar experiences.

You can read about other controversies of Hopi sacred objects in Tony Hillerman's novels, especially *Talking God*. The plot involves the Smithsonian Museum in Washington DC under criminal investigation by Navajo Tribal Police Lieutenant Joe Leaphorn and Officer Jim Chee, over the museum's possession of the revered mask of Teibichai, or Talking God, and collections of Hopi remains exhumed in archeological excavations.

For the Hopi, that sacred mask on the shelf in the Parisian auction house is considered to be a living spirit. Such masks are supposed to be nurtured and cared for within the Hopi community, otherwise sickness or calamity could fall on that community. The only way these masks could have left the Hopi people was either by theft or clandestine sale. Many Hopi believe that the likely culprits who stole the masks and other sacred objects were Hopi witches who were flaunting their power in the face of tribal taboo.

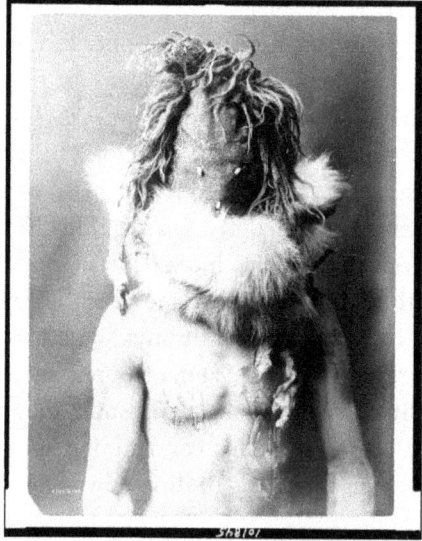

Nayenezgani-Navajo. 1904. Library of Congress, Prints and Photographs Division, Edward S. Curtis Collection, reproduction LC-USZ62-101845.

Three Mesas: Hopi, Arizona — Sacred Masks

Windswept vistas of red and gold sandstone cliffs border Arizona Highway 40, as I drive eastward from Flagstaff. At Winslow, the highway crosses the Little Colorado River. A sign directing me to Highway 87 guides me onto the straight-arrow road for sixty miles to the north to the Hopi Nation.

As I approach the three principal Hopi mesas, height and distance are deceptive. The road ends at Second Mesa, at Highway 264, which connects the villages of First, Second and Third Mesa. To my right a vast cornfield spreads out on desert sand. I park the car and walk out into the field. No fences. Hopis hate fences. Boots sink slightly into loamy, soft sand. Ripe heads of corn swell out of thick green stalks.

In this matriarchal culture, Hopi women protectively store the seed corn, which is blessed in the kivas before planting. A designated elder carefully marks the calendar, watching the cycles of the moon. At the right time, seeds are planted. Antique cottonwood sticks, weathered by years of use, probe openings into the soil. These are holy prayer sticks, potent with fertile powers. Cracked, callused hands drop seeds into each receptive hole—the womb of Mother Earth. After germination, Hopi farmers shield the plants from the intense sun with flat rocks propped up with sticks. And there is singing, always prayerful singing. Just as Anglos speak of talking to plants to encourage their growth, Hopis have prayed over their little corn-children for hundreds of years.

Two red-tail hawks hover high above, shrieking as I walk among the mature corn stalks. Wind suddenly whips up a cloud of sand, stinging my face. I slowly open my eyes and see the wind moving through the cornfield. Long, wispy leaves of cornstalk reach out, sway, and touch the earth like Hopi maidens dancing. I hear singing prayers.

Heavy shadows pass over me, blotting out the sun. A thick thundercloud approaches. Thunder rumbles, the earth quivers. The kachina spirits are coming, bringing the rain that nurtures the corn. Farming in this desert sand with hands, prayer sticks and prayers for rain, is an act of faith.

I return to the car and continue right on the Hopi reservation highway leading to First Mesa, passing a village of square adobe homes. Drying corn ears, tied to string, hang like a colorful necklace from mesquite rafters: blue corn, red corn, white corn, yellow corn: representing the four cardinal sacred directions.

I have an appointment at eleven this morning to meet Susan at the First Mesa Walpi Community Center. Walpi is the oldest Hopi settlement.

It is without running water or electricity. Imagine the effort to climb down rocky trails to fetch water from the stream far below! As the steep access road climbs, I realize how this landscape deceives my senses of height and distance. When I get to the top, I am over six-thousand feet above sea level. As I gaze at the highway below, I feel as though I am on a flat flying saucer hovering over the land. Contributing to this odd feeling is the fact that Walpi and the other villages are among the oldest continuously inhabited places in North America.

The doorway of one crumbling adobe home is blocked with debris. Is it abandoned? Next door, a modern cinder-block home is decorated with colorful curtains. Corn ears and red peppers hang from the rafters.

Susan guides my walk through the village. Dogs bark. Children laugh and play somewhere. Behind the houses, the mesa cliff drops away; there are no fences to keep you from falling into the valley. With a soft, measured voice, Susan shares a narrative about the village and her people. I am careful about asking too many questions. We pass a kiva ceremonial site, a cracked cottonwood ladder sticking out of the hole that leads down into the sacred chamber. The kiva is covered with thick logs of wood, some of them burned. "Was there a fire here?" I ask. Susan's quiet voice answers: "Those are from the Christian mission church, burned in 1680 during the revolt of our people against the Spanish."

It is clear that there is a diverse and thriving artistic community at work here. A potter is removing a pot from an earthen kiln, the curing had been done in steaming sheep dung overnight. A silversmith can be seen through a doorway working carefully at a table. A man wearing a bright red headband weaves a blanket. I speak with a woman who is painting an oval pot with a yucca fiber brush: "How do you find the inspiration for your designs?" Sometimes, images come clearly in her dreams and she is also inspired as she sits among the rocks and trees when she goes down to fetch water. The cottonwoods speak to her and the rocks each have their special place in the landscape. The painter clearly has the intense spiritual awareness of all things, animate and inanimate, being filled with spirit presences that we can commune with.

In my visits to the Hopi I have seen that there is a definite reticence about sacred things, especially when it comes to descriptions of rituals and ceremonies. Clan relationships are more powerful than blood ties. Even husbands and wives of different clans will not discuss their clan's traditions with the other.

Three Mesas: Hopi, Arizona—Sacred Masks

During the last century, American and European anthropologists would camp out, living among the Hopi, sometimes for decades, slowly building trust. Over time, secrets about kiva ceremonies were revealed. Researchers used this information to write dissertations, books and to give lectures. The sacred was harvested to foster academic reputations. The problem for the Hopi is that talking about sacred things to people not of your clan, not of your people, dilutes the spiritual potency of these rites. Today, among the Hopi there is strong resistance to discussing their religion among non-Hopi.

As I walk in the Walpi pueblo, I recognize a tall stone column that appeared in several Edward Curtis photos, the backdrop for the famous kachina dances. While European interlopers tried to suppress these dances in the early years, today Hopi freely celebrate these rituals. It is believed that between December and June the kachinas journey from their home beneath the San Francisco Peaks near Flagstaff, to the Hopi Mesas. Different Hopi clans offer kachina dances, which are prayer rituals inviting these spirits of ancestors and the natural world to bring blessings and rain to the people. Kachina dancers must enter the ritual in a state of purity. When they don the sacred masks, they are possessed by the kachina spirit and become that spirit. This is one reason why putting the masks up for auction in France—or anywhere, is such a devastating travesty: the masks are spirit presences that are alive and must be nurtured and protected. Their theft and their abuse harm the Hopi people.

I am standing near the cliff behind the Walpi Community Center. There is a drop of thousands of feet to the cornfields below. I see a cinderblock home with a porch with a wooden railing facing the mesa. I see a girl and her dog sitting on the porch and I remember a story from *The Spiritual Life of Children* by the child psychologist Robert Coles.

Robert Coles had a natural ability to establish a rapport with children so that they would open up about their lives. In earlier books, he revealed the haunting poverty of Black children in the South, which inspired Kennedy and Johnson to the War on Poverty of the 1960s. In *The Spiritual Life of Children* Coles helps children from different world religions to share their spiritual experiences. One of these encounters is with Natalie, the Hopi girl.

Robert Coles sits with ten-year-old Natalie as they gaze out over cornfields toward Walpi Mesa. He notices that she often seems in an altered state as his tape-recorder picks up the narrative. She seems captivated by the

Desert Spirit Places

land and sky above and the whole world around her. As they talk, she notices a pair of hawks hovering above them. She senses their hungry search for prey, the feel of the wind lifting their wings and their watchfulness of Natalie and Coles. Her gaze returns to the mesa high above her home.

> I think of the mesa a lot. It is where our people live, who are gone, and my mother was taken there when she was little, and she has taken me there and so I think a lot about the mesa, a lot. I visit it in my thoughts, and I meet our ancestors. They give me a blanket and they hold me and they point to the sky and say there are more up there–our ancestors. I will be sitting near a window and I pray to our ancestors and I see them. I sit. I close my eyes. I let myself join our people. I talk with them.[2]

The narrative continues, as Natalie shares a vision of one day when a great circle will enfold and unite her people on the sacred mesa.

> I dream of meeting our Hopi ancestors, and we sit together and talk about the time that will come—the time when all of us are together, and the waters of the rivers are full, and the sun has warmed the cold parts of the world, and it has given the really hot part a break, and all the people are sitting in a huge circle, and they are brothers and sisters, everyone! That's when all the spirits will dance and dance, and the stars will dance, and the sun and the moon will dance, and the birds will swoop down and they'll dance, and all people, everywhere, will stand up and dance, and then they'll sit down again in a big circle, so huge you can't see where it goes, how far, if you're standing on the mesa and looking into the horizon, and everyone is happy. No more fights. Fights are a sign that we have gotten lost, and forgotten our ancestors, and are in the worst trouble. When the day comes that we're all holding hands in the big circle—no, not just us Hopis, everyone—then that's what the word "good" means . . . the whole world will be good when we're all in our big, big circle. We're going around and around until we all get to be there![3]

The Hopi believe that living in these ancient pueblos, high on the mesas in northeastern Arizona, the spiritual center of the universe, their rituals and ceremonies are not only for their people, but a vision of peace and harmony for all of us. Such a vision is sacred, it cannot be bought or sold.

2. Coles, *Spiritual Life of Children*, 151.
3. Coles, *Spiritual Life of Children*, 157.

9.

Santa Ana, & Olancha Creek, California —Insane for the Light: Psychosis and Mysticism

Everyone has to have a spirituality and everyone does have one, either a life-giving one or a destructive one. No one has the luxury of choosing here because all of us are precisely fired into life with a certain madness that comes from the gods and we have to do something with that. We do not wake up in this world calm and serene, having the luxury of choosing to act or not to act. We wake up crying, on fire with desire, with madness. What we do with that madness is our spirituality.

—Ron Rolheiser,[1]

The psychotic drowns in the same waters in which the mystic swims with delight.

—Joseph Campbell[2]

"JESUS IS SITTING ON the bench in the waiting room. He wants to talk with you." Bill Wallace, the Parish Office Manager, has a wry smile. The first sips of good coffee were bringing me to consciousness.

"*Yésüs*," I say, in the Spanish pronunciation. It is a common name among our parishioners here in the Logan Barrio of Santa Ana.

"No. *Jesus* is waiting for you." Bill stresses the English pronunciation.

Okay! I open the security door that guards the church offices from the waiting room. I see a slight, heavily bearded white man of about fifty years,

---

1. Rolheiser, *Holy Longing*, 6.
2. Quoted in Graf, *Psychology of the Future*, 36.

sitting on the bench, his eyes drooping as if he is nodding off. When he sees me his eyes widen with a smile.

"Good morning. Would you like a cup of coffee?" I ask.

"Yes, with four packs of sugar and some cream!" I sit next to him, both holding our coffee. At this point we are companions in waking up for the day. He has been on the street a long time and the smell is strong. He announces, "I am Jesus Christ and I have come to talk with you and give you my blessing." He tells me how he had been sent to bring blessing and to fight the devils in our midst. He tells me what God says to him, especially at night: how clear God's voice is for him. The ideas flood forth, they take flight, they tumble and gyrate, unstoppable. How does he even breathe in this rapid-fire discourse? But after a while, fatigue seems to set in. I make him some hot soup. The intensity fades. He becomes quieter, able to listen to me.

"Where did you spend the night?" I ask.

"Under the carport behind Legal Aid."

I have to go to a meeting. I thank him for visiting me and ask for his blessing.

I was sure to see Jesus here and there; he frequently came to the community lunch that the Catholic Worker community serves in the inner courtyard of the church, and at other times we would greet each other as we passed on a busy city street.

But the next time was not so pleasant. Jesus was panicked and frightened. Demonic voices assaulted him. He asked me to pray that God would drive these evil voices out of him. We seem to have built a measure of trust—enough for him to allow me to get the County mental health team to come by and do an assessment. He went off with them, medications were given at some point and a plan made to get him off the street and into a shelter where he stayed for a few nights. But then he escaped back to the streets and stopped taking the medications.

I remember it was March, during Lent. I arrived for the early morning Mass, parking at the Jack-in-the-Box diner behind the church. Several police cars were in the lot, a huddle of officers. I approached them to find out what was going on, and they nodded toward a small patch of grass. A yellow tarpaulin covered the body. It was Jesus. We later found out that he had suffered some kind of seizure and had died in the night. I asked the officers if I could pray for him. I knelt beside him, my knees soaking in the wet grass. Thick raindrops pattered on the heavy shroud. I never did learn his real name.

This memory was bubbling up into consciousness last night, after I returned from the World Religions class I teach at Saddleback College. I had presented the first lecture and discussion on Hinduism, beginning with an exploration of mysticism. It is a very bright, vocal class this semester. One student asked "What is the difference between mystical experience and schizophrenia or psychosis?" We pondered that question over the next half hour, and the energetic dialogue echoed into my last thoughts before sleep. When I woke up this morning, a clear picture of Jesus popped into my head.

In his *Varieties of Religious Experience*, William James explores a continuum of mystical consciousness from the non-religious, to ecstatic religious experiences. He presents these four characteristics:

Noetic: not a "peak experience" but a life-changing encounter. Life is never the same after this.

Ineffable: the experience defies expression. Due to its subjective nature, the experience is much like a state of feeling

Transient: the experience quickly fades. It is hard to recall the details of the encounter. They remain just out of reach. But some memory content always remains, and this can be used to "modify the inner life of the subject between the time of their recurrence."

Passive experience: Even though many people actively study and/or practice techniques to produce mystical states of consciousness, once it occurs, the mystical experience seems to happen without their will, coming as a surprise when a person least expects it.

The Anglican mystic Evelyn Underhill adds to these defining characteristics of mysticism another quality:

> Direct intuition or experience of God: A mystic is a person who has, to a greater or lesser degree, such a direct experience—one whose religion and life are centered, not merely on an accepted belief or practice, but on that which the person regards as firsthand personal knowledge.[3]

As we enter the world of religious traditions, I always warn my students, culturally attached as they are to Enlightenment philosophy and the scientific method (part of a Westerner's mental DNA), that they should be

---

3. Underhill, *Mystics of the Church*, 3.

aware of their inbuilt skepticism of ecstatic religious experience. As Max Weber observed, the West has demystified our spiritual heritage.

In a vein complementary to William James, in order to create a secular measure of mystical experience, the American psychologist Abraham Maslow writes about "peak-experience," presenting a continuum of characteristics that have to do with the phenomenon. He arrives at the psychologically important conclusion that these experiences facilitate a sense of integration within an individual. Published in 1970, his book on this subject is called, *Religious Aspects of Peak-Experiences*, in which the happiness of a person (i.e. how happy a person can be or become) is brought under scrutiny.

And an academic take on the nature of happiness and its conjunction with religious awareness and sometimes religious mysticism, is not restricted to the psychological. For example, the sociologist and novelist, Father Andrew Greely, and the Zen scholar and Jesuit, Father William Johnston speak to us from their far-ranging personal experiences: they affirm again and again that at the core of mystical experiences is the encounter with love, which brings great joy.

As we study Buddhism and Hinduism, my students learn that the mystic moves from an awareness that life is transient and impermanent. From the awakening of the soul, through various vehicles such as yoga and meditation, quieting the mind, breath and body, becoming detached from material things, one may eventually come to the deep place of pure consciousness and union with Ultimate Reality—God.

Kenneth Wapnick, the Freudian psychologist and therapist who came to use Schucman's famo*us A Course In Miracles* as his central text, concludes that there is a final step to this mystical process: usually persons who have a deep, direct, noetic encounter with the Holy are able to re-enter life and integrate the experience of moving from transience to God, into their life with others.

Teresa of Avila, Spanish mystic (1515–1582). Painting by Alonso de Arco. 1700. PD-1923.

But the big question from my students persists: What is the difference between mysticism and psychosis? The answer is subtle but not difficult to explain. Mysticism and psychosis seem to inhabit a similar space, and—

> I suggest that psychosis. . .and profound spiritual experiences which is often described as mysticism, follow a common process which encompasses euphoria, bewilderment and horror in a sequence that is actual for some of the time and potential for others.[4]

In psychosis, the person loses touch with reality and cannot integrate the experience. But, lest this appear too glib, I agree that such an answer gives rise to further questions;—Is there such a thing as objective reality?—Is Reality the same on Tuesday as it was on Monday?—Ultimately, how can we distinguish the Demonic and the Holy? In sorting all this out, Dr. Tomas Agosin, who was a psychiatrist in the Department of Psychiatry at Albert

4. Stahlman, "Relationship between Schizophrenia and Mysticism."

Einstein College of Medicine in New York, shares these helpful contrasts between psychosis and mysticism:

1. Similarities between psychotic and mystical experiences:

Intense subjectivity: the inward focus is so strong that the outside world is unimportant.

Noetic: this is an important experience where special knowledge may be revealed.

Loss of self-object boundaries: boundaries between self and the outer world can be blurred; a feeling of unity with nature, other persons and the universe.

Distortion of time sense: the present moment becomes the one reality.

Perceptual changes: perceptions intensify with hallucinations and visions.

Intense affective experiences: ecstatic emotions, contrasting experiences of fear/awe/dread with deep longing/love/ecstasy (see Rudolph Otto's *The Idea of the Holy.*)

Attempt at renewal and healing: the mystic encounters an expanded consciousness, deep connections with all aspects of life. The psychotic has come to a blockage in his or her life and the way forward is through radical inner change.

Altered states of consciousness.

2. Differences between psychotic and mystical experiences:

Attachment to the world: the mystic becomes less attached to the world, seeing its impermanent nature. The psychotic detaches from the world to focus completely on what is going on within; ego boundaries dissolve, emotions can change quickly; diminishing sense of connection to the outer world.

Self-image: the mystic reduces focus on self, centering on the vast, expansive world/universe. "The psychotic sees him/herself as omnipotent and omniscient. There is a great increase in self-centeredness, with a feeling of being all-important. He/she is the center of the world, and only he/she is sufficiently important to matter."

Serenity: the mystic is connected with the Holy/Ultimate Reality, which gives peace and serenity. The psychotic, because of the emotional and mental chaos, is possessed by fear and anxiety.

Change: is the new reality for the mystic. The psychotic fears change, because it increases fear and anxiety.

Hallucinatory experiences: the mystic encounters radiant light, "superior beings" and enchanting beauty in nature. The psychotic has auditory hallucinations that are frightening and negative.

Dr. Agosin concludes:

> The mystical experience leaves the mystic more connected and involved in the world. He/she expands his/her capacity to love and to serve. The mystic becomes more appreciative of the beauty and the miracle of life. The mystical experience leaves the individual with a feeling of reverence for all life, embracing every aspect of life and death as sacred.
>
> Psychosis unfortunately most often leaves the person more self-centered. It narrows his/her possibilities of connection with the world because the psychotic needs to protect him/herself from the anxiety that such a connection produces. The psychotic reduces his/her capacity to love because he/she cannot forget him/herself. The psychotic spends so much energy on survival that there is little psychic energy left for more.[5]

Many times, we don't know what is happening within a person until after his or her unusual or extraordinary experience can be reflected upon. Through the help of science today, there is compassionate help for those struggling with mental illness. Coupled with this, it is clear that even within or perhaps because of secularization, we who live in Western culture are in a time of a Great Awakening, of spiritual seeking. All of which certainly helps in distinguishing between the mystical and the psychotic.

I am climbing the twisting cow trail through dense creosote bushes along Olancha Creek in the Eastern Sierra. Ahead of me is stunning Olancha Peak in the Sierra Nevada (pictured on the label of those Crystal Geyser water bottles). Owens Lake is below and behind me. I love the desert—it's resilience, the clarity, the quiet, the sensible pace. By definition, the desert in general and the American Southwest in particular can be seen as the

---

5. Agosin, "Mysticism and Psychosis."

antithesis of civilization, its culture is inchoate. Yet you find John the Baptist and Simon Stylites and the Pilgrim of the Steppes and the ascetic of the Hindu Kush, spending spiritually important time wherever they can find desert space. They leave behind the family and the city and the creature comforts. And the people of the city call them mad.

But all the time of my climb up Olancha Creek, the inner voice speaks in an unhappy mantra: "I shouldn't be here. I should be home with my family. This is selfish of me to be here on this desert retreat."

That was fifteen years ago. Erik had finished another long cycle of seizures, vomiting, hardly eating or drinking over many days, ending up with a week in hospital. Jan and I were shell-shocked numb, drained by another emotional rollercoaster. Another chapter in the saga of horrific struggles of our son had ended; some sense of stability was with us for a while, but for how long? Things quickly change.

I had planned this retreat for several months, but I really should have canceled the whole thing. The more I think about it, the more I miss my family. I want to hold Erik on my lap and love him. I am at the end of my emotional rope again. This horror movie is stuck on replay. Where can I find a hope to hang on to?

I am breathless as I climb; the altitude is getting me. I must stop frequently to catch my breath, lungs burning; got to wait for that beating heart to slow down. I finish a third bottle of water—ironically, as Olancha Creek gurgles over rocks and boulders right next to me. Over several hours of hiking and climbing (I lose all sense of time out here) the brain shifts into neutral, the nagging voices vanish, only the sound of wind whistling through the creosote and the rushing creek. The spine of California, the Sierra Nevada looms closer and closer now, blanketed with thick snow. I begin truly to see the colors around and ahead of me; late afternoon sun reflects rose and amber on the mountains, a golden sheen on the rocks ahead. Such beauty! Stop, stop and take this in! I seem to be completely alone. Is this madness? The sun is a like a gentle heat lamp enveloping me with warmth. My emptied mind opens to phrases bubbling up from—Where? "The Lord takes pleasure in those who fear him, in those who trust in his constant love." (Psalm 147). The gospel song, Leaning on the Everlasting Arms. Is this madness? Is this the endorphins from a long, grueling hike? I feel alive.

God is here. God's love is here. I am remembering the times in the past when God was there, when I was at the end of my rope and hope.

I pray.

Santa Ana, & Olancha Creek, California

> *Thank you, God, for the doctors and nurses who cared for Erik. Thank you for the medicine. Thank you for Jan who is my teammate is this battle for Erik's life. I know we are well past the predictions of his lifespan, but he is with us. Every day is a gift. Thank you, Lord. Thank you for this beautiful place, for your love for me.*

Walking in this desert place, I have holy help in shaking off the dark voices of despair and confusion and in opening my heart to the eternal, loving Presence that is always with me and you—even though we forget.

Father Ron Rolheiser, who is both a friend and mentor, reminds me:

> All of us have our own form of psychosis, of mental illness, of personal sickness, woundedness, dysfunctional history, idiosyncrasy, and plain quirks which distance us from each other. It is not a question of: Are we alienated? It is only a question of: In what ways are we alienated? All of us, as Thoreau says, live lives of quiet desperation and, I might add, of not-so-quiet frustration. All of us spend most of our lives waiting for something else to happen to us. Ninety-nine per center of our lives are spent in a restlessness of one form or the other, waiting for a fuller moment.[6]

I pray.

> *May my testimonies of encounters with God's consolation encourage you to continue your pilgrimage in hope, grounded in gratitude for all those times in the past when God's love enfolded and guided you.*

---

6. Rolheiser, "In Exile."

10.

Mystery Valley, Navajo Nation —The Huge Hogan

Father Brad: "How do you know when you are in a sacred place?"
Harry Nez: "Wherever I am at this moment is a sacred place. The sacred is all around us."

FINE RED, POWDERY DESERT dust covers the tires of the Ford Bronco up to the hub caps. If we stop on this road we will be stuck. Our Navajo/Diné guide, Don Mose, keeps the car moving forward at a fast pace as Janice and Erik and I bounce up and down in our seats and frantically lurch left and right. Erik is laughing up a storm.

The road into remote Mystery Valley is crisscrossed with side roads and desert washes. If it were me navigating we would be lost in minutes, but Don Mose knows what he's doing and nonchalantly keeps up the conversation as we bounce along.

I first greeted Don in Monument Valley, Utah, north of Mystery Valley, at the meeting place for Navajo Spirit Tours. A Diné guide is required in order to enter the restricted area into Mystery Valley. "Ya'at'eeh abini, good morning!"

"Very good. Yes, good morning!"

Which started him into a story about his many years teaching the Navajo/Diné language at Monument Valley High School. "You know, our language is the second-most-difficult language to learn, next to Chinese. It is difficult teaching the young people, as you can't get them away from their cell phones."

"At Goulding's Trading Post this morning I said 'Ahéhee,' Thank you," I replied. "The lady corrected my pronunciation, telling me that what I had actually said was, "I am married!" At least this was not as bad as some of the mispronunciations I made when I first celebrated mass in Spanish. At the time of Communion, instead of saying, "Los Dones de Dios para el Pueblo de Dios—The Gifts of God for the People of God," I said "Las Donas de Dios—The Donuts of God . . ."

Nevertheless, my attempt at the Diné language was reaching out to Don Mose, and I could see that we had made a connection.

Author with Don Mose at Skull Rock, Mystery Valley, Utah. 2017. Photo by Janice Karelius.

Desert Spirit Places

A faint trail on the right brings the vehicle through dense juniper and pinyon pine and what looks like the end of the road: a steep granite shelf jutted upward before us. "Time to engage first gear, four-wheel drive," announces Don Mose. "I hope this works. I wouldn't dare do this in my own car!" And remarkably, the weather-beaten Ford slowly ascends the rocky face, our guide expertly navigating the fissures and crannies to a level place high above. He stops the car and tells us it is safe to step outside.

In the distance is the iconic landscape of Monument Valley, which is called in Diné, *Tsé Bii Ndzisgaii*, The Valley of the Rocks. Sandstone buttes erupt here and there. In my mind I see John Wayne riding atop a stagecoach here—John Ford's *Stagecoach* of 1939 was the actor's breakout movie. Monument Valley is the main player in a dozen iconic Westerns. Here, nothing seems too long ago, the past is present. In fact, the Navajo Tribal Park has its own time zone. The ruins of villages and the rock art remind us of the ancient people who once lived here, and bring them to the present.

Don Mose finds a way down from the precipice and soon we are on another sandy road winding through buttes and sandy clumps of yellow-blooming rabbit brush. Some divine hand has shaped the sandstone cliffs with arches and deep-set crevices.

We come to a hidden corner of high red cliffs and, in the distance, a breathtaking sight: a well-preserved Anasazi ruin can be seen. It is built partly in a cave. This particular vestige is known as the Square House Ruin. As we walk towards it, the stone walls of the ruin glisten in the sunlight, looking as though they were constructed recently rather than a thousand years ago.

Janice, Erik and I stand with Don Mose upon a mound of the fine red sand that wind and rain removed from the red cliffs above us. "This was all covered by a great ocean millions of years ago," says Don Mose. The inveterate teacher makes a small mound of the sand and compresses it with his hands. He takes a cup of water and pours it around the mound, until the sides fall away. He gently removes some of the sand and there it is: a miniature of the gigantic buttes around us. "This is how the wind and rain slowly carved these wonderful buttes around us."

Haunting images of the vast expanse and geological wonders of the Colorado River Plateau, which includes Monument Valley and Mystery Valley, have excited Anglo-American imaginations for more than a century.

Mystery Valley, Navajo Nation — The Huge Hogan

Although for these visitors it seemed to be a virgin, undeveloped landscape ready to be explored, studied and interpreted, for thousands of years this part of Creation has been sacred land for the First People, which includes the ancestral Puebloan-Anasazi, Ute, Hopi and Navajo.

Thomas J. Harvey captures what this particular desert space means to both the Native and Anglo-American cultures in his book *Rainbow Bridge to Monument Valley: Making the Modern Old West*. In his review of Anglo-American explorations, he presents the idea of American Occidentalism. In these nineteenth- and twentieth-century expeditions, using colors such as geology and anthropology, the Anglo culture painted its own picture, its own construct of the American Southwest, on what the interlopers in their ignorance took to be a blank canvas.

> Using the term "American Occidentalism," however permits the discourses and practices that produced the twentieth-century Southwest as an exotic space juxtaposed to modern life to be identified within their particular cultural context and historical moment. Like (Edward) Said's Orientalists, American Occidentalists were, as they moved through Native spaces, engaged in a form of imperialism. Yet, the other aspect of this Occidentalism was that it exposed a hollow longing, an unremembered past, an emptiness of the heart of the very culture that modernization had helped to produce.[1]

These phrases "hollow longing," "unremembered past" and "emptiness of the heart" connect with a central theme of this book: the blessings and productivity of our rationalistic, technological age have left us with a gnawing dissatisfaction and longing for something intangible, but which finds us able to be at home in desert spirit places.

In his famous book, the New York philosopher Marshall Berman reflects:

> It appears that the very process of development, even as it transformed the wasteland into a thriving physical and social space, recreates the wasteland inside of the developer himself.[2]

Driving into Monument Valley yesterday, we had to be vigilant and watchful. As the road took a blind corner, there was a knot of tourists standing right in the middle of the highway gazing at and photographing

---

1. Harvey, *Rainbow Bridge*, 7.
2. Berman, *All That Is Solid*, 5–6.

the massive rocky spires of Monument Valley. They were entranced, quite oblivious to any danger.

The desire to find and live out one's True Self cannot be found in the restless, changing dynamics of modern urban life. The Southwestern desert and its First People feed the search for substantial reality. Time and again, as we watched the faces and behaviors of the hundreds of visitors who arrived at Monument Valley by the hour, we could see them caught up in euphoria and wonder. There is something real, palpably authentic, here in Monument Valley. The ancient ruins, vibrant native culture and geological wonders touch an inner longing in the Anglo-American, European and Asian visitors.

> The exposed land forms created over millennia, the presence of Indians still living in traditional ways, and the location of ruins of now-vanished ancient races contributed to this sense of the Southwest as a storehouse of the past and, therefore, primitive and authentic.[3]

Square House Ruin, Ancient Puebloan, c. 100 CE, Mystery Valley, Utah. Photo by author.

3. Harvey, *Rainbow Bridge*, 9.

Mystery Valley, Navajo Nation — The Huge Hogan

But the Navajo landscape has a story of its own. This is where I believe Don Mose and our guide of two years ago, Harry Nez, are so important. They are evangelists, message-bearers, who take it as their mission to share some of the Diné/Navajo narrative with all these visitors. This land is not a blank canvas only to be interpreted by Anglo-American culture; for thousands of years this has been sacred space for the First Peoples. In the few hours my family spent with Harry Nez and Don Mose in our tours of Monument Valley and Mystery Valley, they were able to open up some of the sacred story of the Diné people.

I kneel with Don Mose in the mound of fine red desert sand. Don is no longer a tour guide but a spiritual teacher. Someone later told me that he was a medicine man (hatalii), one who has been trained in the healing ceremonies. He says,

> Our Diné people do not have a word for religion. I think that for the Anglo-Americans religion it is a separate part of life. But for our people the sacred is everywhere. The world is filled with powerful spirit presences. There are Holy Ones who bring healing and protection. There are dark spirits and witches who seek to bring disharmony, sickness and suffering. What we have to do in our personal life is work at balance and harmony, hozhooji. Walk in beauty. We want to keep our connection with Mother Earth. Here, let me show you about our sacred land.

Don Mose draws the four cardinal points in the sand.

> We have four sacred mountains. Here is Blanca Peak/Dawn, or White Shell Mountain, which is in Colorado. Mount Taylor/Blue Bead, or Turquoise Mountain, in New Mexico is to the south. The San Francisco Peaks/Abalone Shell Mountain are in Arizona to the west, and Hesperus Mountain/Big Sheep Mountain is in Colorado. We remember these sacred directions in the four colors of the corn: blue, white, red and yellow. And see, right here in the middle are the Hopi people.

But what exactly is a sacred place? Editha Watson, who spent much of her life researching and recording especially Navajo culture, has a succinct answer.

Desert Spirit Places

For the Diné people a sacred place is: 1) a location mentioned in

legend; 2) a place where something supernatural has happened; 3) a site from which plants, herbs, minerals and waters possessing healing powers may be taken; and 4) where man communicates with the supernatural world by means of prayers and offerings.[4]

The hogan is the primary dwelling of a Navajo. The Diné belief is that this whole area of Monument Valley is one huge hogan. As in the Diné hogan homes, the door faces east at the visitor's center where I met Don this morning. The center of the great hogan called Monument Valley is the butte behind Goulding's Trading Post, near where we are camping.

Don Mose continues his exposition. "Healing for the Diné is to understand that illness is a dis-ease; something is out of balance which needs to be restored to harmony, and we have many ceremonies that we use to heal people or prevent them from becoming sick. We sing our prayers for healing. I will sing you part of a blessing." He closes his eyes and sings a sacred chant. The holy sound is amplified in this recessed canyon with the ancient ruin looming above us. The wind carries the holy song out over the desert. There is a YouTube recording of Don Mose singing his healing song.[5]

Saint Augustine said: "He or she who sings, prays twice."[6]

---

4. Watson, *Navajo Sacred Places*, 22.

5. "Don Mose—Navajo Spirit tour guide," https://www.youtube.com/watch?v=6rcqwN7-scI.

6. Augustine, *Commentary of Psalm 73*, 1.

Mystery Valley, Navajo Nation — The Huge Hogan

After the singing, I gaze at the land around us: pinyon pine, sagebrush, juniper, pottery shards on the ground, a tiny, ancient corn cob, and crumbling stones that have fallen from the ruins above. This is not dead space filled with ancient debris. This place is alive; the rocks, trees, wind, and ruins are spiritual presences. The ancestral spirits are a communion of saints who can bring peace, harmony and beauty.

It is late afternoon and the crunch of tour buses, the crowds of international travelers and the trains of recreational vehicles have moved on. Some people have settled into hotel rooms, others continue to Kayenta or Flagstaff. Tranquility settles over the visitor's center and the Diné View Hotel overlooking Monument Valley. Janice, Erik and I sit on the patio behind the hotel. The valley drops dramatically below us and in the distance are iconic buttes, much photographed. We are by ourselves on the patio, awaiting Nature's show. The sun is setting in the west. The dull red-brown texture of the majestic buttes begins to change into a brilliant red. Then, for just five minutes the buttes change to a luminous gold. I look quickly around me. Is no one else catching this? What a wonder! The sun is setting. The buttes become deep purple. As darkness descends, they become shadowy silhouettes. This is no fresh canvas only recently painted by European culture. This is an ancient canvas on which the Creator paints wonder and glory every day.

Janice and Erik Karelius, Poverty Hills, California. 2016. Photo by author.

11.

Poverty Hills, California
—Digging for Treasure

[George Lewis of Independence reports] the richest gold ledge ever found in this or any other country. Every piece of the quartz is said to show free gold.
—*Inyo Independent*, June 7, 1895

For where your treasure is, there your heart will be also.
—Matthew 6:21

THE VOLCANIC LAVA FLOWS towards me in a slow, luminescent river of crimson and yellow, halting briefly, building up mounds of molten rock, exploding, sending meteor-like projectiles towards me. I can sense the intense heat and the choking sulfur fumes. I stand upon a mountain of smoking volcanic debris, looking across at the volcano. My imagination rests and I return to the present moment, as I gaze across the Owens Valley toward the Inyo Mountains to the east. The volcano and the lava flow are frozen in time, a rugged sculpting of an event that took place two thousand years ago.

I am standing at a high point in Poverty Hills, fifteen miles north of Independence, California. Mount Whitney is behind me and Highway 395 is far below. All around are the foothills created by several great volcanoes that have covered the desert with a vast lava flow and clusters of volcanic rock. It is this volcanic activity of the distant past that cooked precious metals and forced the liquid through cracks in the quartz to become veins of treasure imbedded is these Poverty Hills and the Inyo Mountains. The history of the Owens Valley from 1860 onwards includes treasure seekers searching for gold and silver. Today as I hike the old mining trails that wind up and down these hills, I can easily identify dark galena rocks, the most common ore of lead. Usually they hold some crystals of silver. With a magnifying glass I can see specks of gold there too.

Fifteen miles north of Independence, California, Highway 395 crosses Elna Road which leads to the Owens River. At that intersection you can turn left toward the Sierra Nevada and into the Poverty Hills. High clearance SUVs do best here. At a turn in the road, on your right, you will see a fine example of a rock-walled miner's cabin. The walls are intact, protected by a tin roof. A stove pipe projects from the back of the cabin. When you enter, you can see how the miner chiseled into the base granite rock and created something that looks like a fireplace but which may have been some kind of primitive furnace to process ore samples.

Returning to the dirt road, I decide to leave my car and walk up the hill. The road climbs steeply, and to my right and left I can see evidence of "rat hole" exploration pits.

Let's practice some elementary mining archaeology together. As we walk the winding uphill trail, we will need to stop and rest occasionally as we adjust to the altitude. At the top it is 4000 feet above sea-level. Where do you think the miners searched for gold and silver? Look for mounds of excavated dirt. The larger the mound, the deeper the dig. You will find some open mine tunnels, which are called adits. For your safety, stay clear of these. Where do you think the miner would have put up a tent cabin? Look for leveled space at the base of a hillock and rummage through the debris there: bottles, cans, nails. If you find a square-sided nail, you will know that this site was from before the year 1900. Where do you think the outhouse would have been? Look for pits with lots of tin cans and broken bottles around the excavation. I can see bottle hunters have been digging here for antique bottles to sell over the internet. As you explore, you will see some of the equipment used in the expensive mining enterprise: heavy cables for hoisting the ore or supporting a tramway, rails for ore cars, iron pipes for bringing water from Birch Creek, three miles to the west.

George Lewis' discovery in 1895 of a vein of gold six-inches wide, the ore being worth about eighty dollars a ton, sparked a gold rush into the Poverty Hills. But the "million-dollar" discovery soon faded away.

In 1902 Alonzo Casler of Ohio bought several mines in this part of the Poverty Hills that we are currently exploring. As his Buckeye Mine project developed, Casler invested thousands of dollars. The ore turned out to be of low grade and the most economical way to get at it was by quarrying with a steam shovel. A mill had to be constructed near the mines to lower the cost of processing the ore. Over $100,000 was invested in building the mill and piping water over the Poverty Hills from Birch Creek. But the mill was fully operational for only about a year, and after that just intermittently during World War I.

Walk with me towards the hillside southwest of the dirt road leading into the Poverty Hills, across from the stone cabin, and we will find extensive ruins of the mill for the Buckeye, Never Rest, and New Era mines.

The historian, Janice Emily Bowers writes:

> At the mill site: concrete footings for mill equipment, stone cabin with corrugated metal roof; concrete pad for small building; abundant detritus including milled lumber, metal cable, disassembled telephone poles, water heaters, vehicle gasoline tanks, metal buckets, etc. At the powerhouse site: cement walls along ditch in bottom of Birch Creek ravine...[1]

These Poverty Hills and the Inyo Mountains to the east are pockmarked with hundreds of mines, following the trail of lust for gold and silver. But the mines never lasted. More often than not investors would spend more money than would ever come out of the mine. Just a whispering hint of another strike would set off a frenzy of treasure-seeking, soon followed by dashed hopes.

The stories make excellent material for Westerns, many of which were filmed thirty miles south in the Alabama Hills, between 1925 and the present. But this land is not only a backdrop, a place for the passive viewer, for as you hike in the breathtaking beauty of the landscape, immerse yourself in it geological wonders, the silence and solitude work on our inner selves, our souls, imbuing us with an ancient, solid beauty and peace, penetrating, soothing our busy minds with their tasks and concerns of the past and the future. The silence and solitude in this desert place pulls us down into a deeper space, asking us: where are you searching for treasure?

We are forever restless and searching for someone or something that will bring us a sense of security, peace, serenity. But no one and nothing seems to satisfy. We are haunted by endless dissatisfaction. I can divert my dissatisfaction by working harder, jumping into new projects, or by taking pills or drinking booze to give me a buzz or ephemeral tranquility. But

1. Bowers, *Fish Springs and Black Rock*, 247.

none of that lasts. Yet if you walk this vast land for any amount of time, the silence and solitude will work on you just as the wind and sand and water work on the boulders and mountains. You have nothing to fear in walking here in silence. I welcome the chance. My years of walking in these desert spaces have brought me to the Treasure—a Benevolent Presence.

Ron Rolheiser writes:

> At the center of our experience lies an incurable dis-ease, a disquiet, a restlessness, a loneliness, a longing, a yearning, a desire, an ache for something we can never quite name. For what are we longing? What would satisfy our restless energy? Anne Frank, in her famous Diary, asks exactly this question:
>
> 'Today the sun is shining, the sky is a deep blue, there is a lovely breeze and I am longing—so longing—for everything. To talk, for freedom, for friends, to be alone. And I do so long . . . to cry! I feel as if I am going to burst, and I know it would get better with crying; but I can't. I'm restless, I go from room to room, breathe through the crack of a closed window, feel my heart beating, as if it was saying, "can't you satisfy my longing at last?" I believe that it is spring within me; I feel that spring is awakening. I feel it in my whole body and soul. It is an effort to behave normally, I feel utterly confused. I don't know what to read, what to write, what to do, I only know that I am longing.'[2]

What is the treasure that would satisfy our restless hearts?

There is a Hasidic story told of a man named Isaac who lived in Cracow. He was very poor, so when he dreamed three times in a row about a great treasure buried under a bridge in the distant city of Prague, he set out on a journey to find it. But when he arrived in Prague, he discovered that the place he had seen in his dream was patrolled day and night by the king's guards. He circled the spot, watching it from a distance, until finally the guards noticed him. When the captain called to Isaac and demanded to know what he was doing there, Isaac told him about the dream. "You mean to tell me that you believe in such dreams!" laughed the captain. "If I believed in them, I would have to go all the way to Cracow and find some man named Isaac, because I have dreamed that a great treasure lies buried beneath his bed!" Isaac thanked the captain, returned home, pushed aside his bed, and dug up the treasure that had been there all along.

---

2. Rolheiser, "Longing Is Our Spiritual Lot."

Desert Spirit Places

For forty years I have made spiritual retreats to the desert spaces of the Owens Valley, Death Valley, and other spirit places in Arizona, Utah, Nevada and New Mexico. I find these words from Ron Rolheiser helpful as an invitation to those who seek spiritual treasures:

> The desert does this for you. It empties you. Hence it is not a place wherein you can decide how you want to grow and change, but is a place that you undergo, expose yourself to, and have the courage to face. The idea is not so much that you do things there, but that things happen to you while there—silent, unseen, transforming things. The desert purifies you, almost against your will, through God's efforts. In the desert, what really occurs is a cosmic confrontation between God and the devil; though this happens within and through you. Your job is only to have the courage to be there. The idea is that God does the work, providing you have the courage to show up.[3]

---

3. Rolheiser, "Desert, a Place of Preparation."

12.

Sunset Crater, Arizona—Eyes to See

Sometimes you can see a whole lot of things just by looking.
—Yogi Berra

Nature gave the word glory a meaning for me. If nature had never awakened certain longings in me, huge areas of what I mean by the love of God would never have existed.
—C.S. Lewis[1]

"You're next, Father Karelius!" the nurse barked as she wheeled another patient into surgery.

Warm blankets cocooned me. The IV dripped and my heart raced. Eye surgery! It was hard for me to conceive of how they could cut into my eye and operate on it. I had had several serious surgeries involving long stays at Cedars Sinai Hospital in Los Angeles, but eye surgery—what would that be like? This is the "window to the soul," quite apart from it being a delicate and dreadfully vulnerable part of my body. One of my students at Saddleback College who was in the nursing program confessed that she would trade eye surgery for gastro-intestinal surgery any day. Eye surgery: too gross! Help!

I am wheeled into the operating room, and our friend, Dr. Paul Prendiville, speaks in a low, calming voice. Anesthesia takes effect and I am watching a kaleidoscope of vibrant, flaming colors turning and twisting, like a Tibetan mandala. The movement of crystalline colors slows, and I hear voices again: Dr. Paul and my wife, first in the distance, then very

---

1. Lewis, *Four Loves*, 40.

close. I awaken with a patch over my eye. Everything was successful. In a week I would see again.

The poet and mystic Annie Dillard writes:

> When her doctor took her bandages off and led her into the garden, the girl who was no longer blind saw "the tree with the lights in it." It was for this tree I searched through the peach orchards of summer, in the forest of fall and down winter and spring for years. Then one day I was walking along Tinker Creek thinking of nothing at all and I saw the tree with the lights in it. I saw the backyard cedar where the mourning doves roost charged and transfigured, each cell buzzing with flame. I stood on the grass with the lights in it, grass that was wholly fire, utterly focused and utterly dreamed. It was less like seeing than like being for the first time seen, knocked breathless by a powerful glance. The flood of fire abated, but I am still spending the power. Gradually, the lights went out in the cedar, the colors died, the cells unflamed and disappeared. I was still ringing. I had been my whole life a bell, and never knew it until at that moment I was lifted and struck.[2]

There is a seeing that involves the delicate body parts that create the eye. There is a deeper seeing, called illumination, that is an inner, mystical seeing that cannot be conjured, mentally directed or manipulated.

Annie Dillard again:

> . . . the pearl may be found, it may not be sought. The literature of illumination reveals this above all: although it comes to those who wait for it, it is always, even to the most practiced and adept, a gift and total surprise.[3]

One of the reasons I have written these chapters on spirit places in the desert is to invite you to enter, walk, wait, and watch. I have found that with fatigue from long hikes during desert retreats and several days of silence and solitude, *"Aha! moments"* of intuitive insight flash into my consciousness. This Southwestern landscape is a doorway into mystery and wonder. The gift often involves a Benevolent Presence offering peace, joy, hope and love.

Interstate 40 out of Kingman, Arizona, flies across high desert chaparral into an ocean of sagebrush. It twists and climbs through volcanic and granite mountain passes, heading east toward Flagstaff. Though Janice,

---

2. Dillard, *Pilgrim at Tinker Creek*, 33–34.
3. Dillard, *Pilgrim at Tinker Creek*, 34.

Sunset Crater, Arizona—Eyes to See

Erik and I travel this route every October, I am still at first astonished at what I see: a rainbow of wildflowers bursting from the sandy soil, violet puffs of Arizona lupine, and clusters of white desert chicory and desert sunflowers. Back home in Orange County, the hillsides around our home are blowtorched dry-brown in the absence of rain. But here in Arizona, speeding past ocotillo, cholla and saguaro cactus, cruise control set at 75 miles an hour, I watch the colorful, dramatic landscape flash by like an IMAX movie.

At seven thousand feet the highway straightens. We pass through a windswept plateau of deep green range-grass on which hundreds of sheep and cattle flourish. And there is not a tree in sight.

These desert and mountain journeys through the American Southwest bring us into tremendous open spaces of geological wonder. But after fifty miles or so, the sheer vastness swallows up our vision and everything becomes too-familiar. I confess, I can be walking through the Getty Museum in Los Angeles, trying to slowly savor the colors and textures of great artistic masters. But after a while a malaise and sensory overload possess me. I am done. This same malaise sets in, as we pass through this amazing beauty. I think The English writer G. K. Chesterton knew of this phenomenon when he wrote, "Our perennial spiritual and psychological task is to look at things familiar until they become unfamiliar again."[4]

Seeing means more than having good eyesight. We can do a lot of looking at the world around us without seeing much. Our eyes can be wide open, but we see nothing. How can we look at familiar things until they look unfamiliar again? We need help to see through this familiarity that surrounds us in order to see into wonder.

Guidance comes to me from our disabled adult son Erik, and from the Jewish mystic Martin Buber.

After we set up camp at J&H Campground in Flagstaff, Janice, Erik and I head north on Interstate 89 a few miles to Loop Road, which leads to Sunset Crater Volcano National Monument. We park at the Ranger Station and walk into a pine forest. I hold Erik's hand, as we walk the winding path around dense piles of pine needles. Erik's eyes are unfocused, gazing off into nothing. His significant brain damage from encephalitis in 1987 has meant years of suffering for him and for all of us as we struggle to minimize his seizures. His far-away gaze could be an absence seizure. But as we walk, this handsome young man, mentally four years old within a strapping six-foot adult body, slowly awakens. I pick up a pine cone and he

---

4. Chesterton, *Everlasting Man*, 10.

feels the sticky pitch and the sharp spines and he senses the sweet sap. We walk further into the dense wood. I call his attention to sounds of squirrels fighting over another pine cone, squawky blue jays and the distant yelp of a coyote. "Listen, Erik, what is that? A bird? Squirrels fighting? A coyote calling to her children?" I call Erik's attention to sense, sound, touch, smell and taste and he is becoming more alert, more present to this natural world. As I do this, the familiar sounds and sights become unfamiliar again to me. There is a slowing into which Erik is pulling me, a slowing of time and space. And I am present to him and he to me. We reach the edge of the forest and encounter a vast meadow of wildflowers, clusters of bulbs that have burst into four-foot-high columns of yellow and orange. Erik sees the shapes and colors and begins to walk into the meadow, passing his hands over the tall tubers.

I also found help in seeing nature in a new way from the Jewish mystic Martin Buber and his book *I and Thou (Ich und Dich)*. He shares his personal experience about how encounters with Nature can be transformative and can lead us into deeper communion with each other and God.

Buber contends that we have two ways of connecting with the world around us. The world of reason and science has shaped our consciousness to approach the world around us using the scientific method to collect information, analyze and classify it and to create theories about it. Buber calls this mode "Experience," and we approach creation as an "It," detached from ourselves (as though we were not an integral part of the world). We apply the information we collect to furthering some project or other: falling in love, going to work, feeding the dog. But in this there is a detachment, a distance between us and creation (I-It).

Buber helped me to understand that there is another way to connect with the world around me. He calls this "Encounter," wherein we enter into relationship with the object we see, hear, feel. I believe this is why the setting of the American Southwest is helpful, because the tribal Native American and Hispano traditions invite a porous receptivity to animate what rationalist cultures consider inanimate creation.

Through his personal experience in meditating on a tree, Buber experiences the dissolution of distance between himself and the tree and a merging into oneness.

Sunset Crater, Arizona—Eyes to See

> I consider a tree. I can look on it as a picture: stiff column in a shock of light, or splash of green shot with the delicate blue and silver of the background. I can perceive it as movement: flowing veins on clinging, pressing pith, suck of the roots, breathing of the leaves, ceaseless commerce with earth and air—and the obscure growth itself.[5]

As Buber contemplates the tree and describes its qualities, something changes.

> It can, however, also come about, if I have both will and grace, that in considering the tree I become bound up in relation to it. The tree is no longer an It.[6]

Living only within the world of I-It brings with it negative psychological fallout. You become anxious about the future, you lose a sense of meaning to life, you are chronically dissatisfied. You know the feeling when you awaken at 3 a.m. and can't go back to sleep.

If we allow our porous selves to open up to encounter nature and, like Annie Dillard, we are receptive, the tree with the lights in it may visit us. We cannot force the encounters, but we can prepare ourselves for them. And we can be ready to be changed—fundamentally or slightly, or somewhere in between—by the encounter.

Buber reminds us that all of these encounters are transient and that soon the I-Thou connection will change, by our reflection and analysis, back into I-It. The lasting I-Thou relationship, Buber confesses, is in the state of love and with God. We call this Revelation.

Likely you, and certainly I, visit this Southwestern landscape as children of The Enlightenment. We have been schooled in the I-It world, we have learned to discount mystical and spiritual experience. The gift of this desert land, nature's creatures and the people who have lived here for centuries is that the place will work on your inner self, as patiently as sand and wind wear down a massive granite boulder. If we are open and searching, transformative encounters may visit us.

Here is one memorable encounter related by the psychologist William James.

> I remember the night, and almost the very spot on the hilltop, where my soul opened out into the Infinite, and there was a rushing

---

5. Buber, *I and Thou*, 14.
6. Buber, *I and Thou*, 14.

together of the two worlds, the inner and the outer. It was deep calling unto deep—the deep that my own struggle had opened up within being answered by the unfathomable deep without, reaching beyond the stars. I stood alone with He who had made me, and all the beauty of the world, and love, and sorrow, and even temptation. I did not seek Him, but felt the perfect unison of my spirit with His. The ordinary sense of things around me faded. For the moment nothing but an ineffable joy and exultation remained. It is impossible fully to describe the experience. It was like the effect of some great orchestra when all the separate notes have melted into one swelling harmony that leaves the listener conscious of nothing save that his soul is being wafted upwards, and almost bursting with its own emotion. The perfect stillness of the night was thrilled by a more solemn silence. The darkness held a presence that was all the more felt because it was not seen. I could not anymore have doubted He was there than I was. Indeed, I felt myself to be, if possible, the less real of the two.[7]

I am inviting you into a contemplative awareness. It is not hard to find. In fact, when you walk in these desert spirit places, it will find you. Contemplative awareness is seeing things as they are, resting in the Holy Presence, sitting like an "untrained child," and in a time of no-mind.

Here is a spiritual exercise for you to try out. Find yourself a quiet place during your desert spirit visit—a place where you will be undisturbed. Do this a little before sunset. Have no agenda but to be attentive to the growing darkness. Sit there with the Holy Presence at the setting of the sun. Sit for a full hour.

> Sit in the unrelenting sovereignty of the day's end. Sit in radical obedience to the falling light.[8]

This exercise may more deeply awaken your inner sight for the glory that surrounds us.

---

7. James, *Varieties of Religious Experience*, ch. 3.
8. Rolheiser, "Contemplative Sound Bytes."

13.

North of Santa Fe, New Mexico —The Penitentes

A click; the room was darkened; and suddenly, on the screen above the Master's head, there were the Penitentes of Acoma prostrating themselves before Our Lady, and wailing as John had heard them wail, confessing their sins before Jesus on the Cross, before the eagle image of Pookong. The young Etonians fairly shouted with laughter. Still wailing, the Penitentes rose to their feet, stripped off their upper garments and, with knotted whips, began to beat themselves, blow after blow. Redoubled, the laughter drowned even the amplified record of their groans.

"But why do they laugh?" asked the Savage in a pained bewilderment.

"Why?" The Provost turned towards him a still broadly grinning face. "Why? But because it's so extraordinarily funny."[1]

TRAVELING THE BACK ROADS of New Mexico can be disorienting. The Old Pecos Trail and the Old Santa Fe Trail may well pass through suburban Santa Fe, but before I know it, the road narrows and suddenly becomes a trail winding through six-foot high walls of tumbleweed, sagebrush and mesquite and I am thoroughly lost. I punch my campground destination into Google Maps on the I-phone, and the calming, confident female voice guides me back to where I should be. Amazing.

---

1. Huxley, *Brave New World*, ch. 11.

However, on recent journeys to El Santuario del Chimayo, as country roads wend through Indian pueblos and old Hispano villages, I have twice come to a crossroads where there are no directional signs and where my digital guide goes blank. The soothing voice disappears and the map on the phone makes no sense. As I look back now, I understand: I have entered mystical spiritual territory where I must carefully pick my way intuitively towards my destination. God give me a sign!

On Highway 76 (the High Road to Taos), we are driving north of Santa Fe through the Carson National Forest. On this warm spring day, the dry, thin air is fragrant with the scent of pinyon pine and juniper. There is a village ahead, Las Trampas, and we turn off for breakfast at La Casita Café. Warm fry-bread coated with cinnamon and sugar complement the spicy pinyon coffee. I listen to the conversations around us, English mixed with Spanish. I am fluent in Spanish but have a difficult time understanding much until I catch some antique phases that remind me of the "thees" and "thous" of the old Episcopal Spanish prayer book. The local people are speaking an eighteenth-century Spanish colonial dialect, a vestige of four hundred years of imperial occupation remains in these isolated New Mexican villages.

As we pass the Church of San Jose de Gracia, for some reason my eye catches an obscure square adobe building next door. I later find out it is a *morada*—a sanctuary for the Penitentes or Brothers of Light. For now, I am not particularly intrigued, but that will soon change.

We travel on, looking for some direction toward Chimayo, but an unseen power has again disabled the GPS. We pass through Las Truchas where I recognize the market and other buildings from my favorite Robert Redford film, *The Milagro Beanfield Wars* (1987). I often play the music of the soundtrack; it captures the spiritual power of this place, where villagers regularly consult with santos and angels in their daily life.

–God give us a sign!—And there it is! Just ahead I see four men walking together, barefoot, following a bearded young man, jet-black hair flowing freely to his waist, carrying the heavy beam of a huge wooden cross. This is the midpoint in the holy season of Lent and these are Penitentes walking to Chimayo. If I get out of the car and follow them, I'll be certain to get where I'm going. Just then I hear bells. Church bells. It is noon. Mass has just ended. I must be near my destination.

North of Santa Fe, New Mexico—The Penitentes

The Penitentes of New Mexico, *Los Hermanos de la Fraternidad Piadosa de Nuestro Padre Jesus Nazareno* (the Brothers of the Pious Fraternity of Our Father Jesus the Nazarene), are bread and butter to students of cultural anthropology. Popular media through the years have luridly presented the strange rituals of flagellation and crucifixion. The 1937 film *Lash of the Penitentes*, which is mocked by the Etonian students in Huxley's Brave New World, derides the primitive rituals as "horrible" and "abusive." Perhaps some of the best photographs of the Penitentes in New Mexico were taken by Charles Lummis. In his book *The Land of Poco Tiempo*, he wrote:

> ... so late as 1891 a procession of flagellants took place within the limits of the United States. A procession in which voters of this Republic shredded their naked back with savage whips, staggered beneath huge crosses, and hugged the maddening needles of the cactus.[2]

Lummis had to go to lengths to establish trust between himself and members of the Brotherhood so that he would be allowed to photograph these private rituals in the Sangre de Cristo Mountains—after all, these were not papparazzo-snaps that he took. There is irony, then, that his images were used to feed an insensitive and critical Anglo press which fostered a sensational, negative impression of the Penitentes.

Penitentes procession, Taos, New Mexico. C. 1900. Library of Congress.

2. Lumnis, *Land of Poco Tiempo*, 56.

The curious rituals attracted many spiritual seekers throughout the twentieth century. Visitors to New Mexico were properly enchanted by the Hispano-Pueblo culture, but all too often when they reported to the outside world their experiences with these local spiritual rituals, they spoke as though they had found a realm disconnected from reality.

In his *The Sacred World of the Penitentes*, the scholar Alberto Pulido shares:

> What is critical to remember is that Lummis's work would establish the framework for the hundreds of popular and scholarly publications that, like his own work, ignored the importance of penitente understanding and thinking about the sacred in their lives.[3]

But the Procession of the Cross which I have just witnessed at the side of the road, is clear evidence of a profound spirituality deeply imbedded within the hearts of the people who live in the pueblos which dot the lands around Sanctuario del Chimayo. The roots of the ascetical practice of flagellation go back more than a thousand years to Spain and Italy, identifying with the Flagellation of Jesus during his Passion. Rigorous ascetical practices were a part of Christian spirituality from the earliest times. For example, the monks of North Africa, Simon Stylites, Anthony of the Desert, among many, influenced Western monasticism in this respect. Eventually the Roman Catholic Church suppressed the practice of bodily mortification in the fourteenth century, but as we shall see, the Church has trouble putting a damper on popular piety. In the sixteenth century, the Protestant Reformer, Martin Luther, when he was a Roman Catholic monk in Erfurt, Germany, had, hanging on the door of his cell, a whip which he used regularly on himself—this was not at all unusual for the times.

The Spanish ascetical traditions traveled to New Mexico. After Mexican Independence in 1821, in an effort to curtail the power of the religious orders, the Church replaced the Franciscan, Jesuit, and Dominican missionaries with diocesan priests. But, as today in Mexico, there were not enough secular priests to go around, and little villages like the ones in the Chimayo area might see a priest only once a year. And that is, more or less, why lay movements such as that which became popularly known as the

---

3. Pulido, *Sacred World of the Penitentes*, 37.

North of Santa Fe, New Mexico—The Penitentes

Penitentes came to fill a spiritual vacuum—some steps removed from the central Church discipline and even doctrine.

The American anthropologist Marta Weigle notes this:

> A century or more of improvisation in religious expressions, necessitated by the lack of ecclesiastics to minister in time of need, and to celebrate the important events of the Christian year, may well have resulted in a varied conglomeration of lay practices, prayers, penances and procession.[4]

With or without clergy, the spirituality of the people did remain vibrant. The men of the villages would band together for mutual support and to encourage and administer community charity. Part of their ritual developed into Walking in the Way of Jesus in his Passion of the Cross. The men would gather in the morada, the simple, windowless, adobe meetinghall (which brings to mind the Hopi and Pueblo kivas, of the same region). Though secrecy was concomitant with the rituals, the village would know when the men were worshipping from the resonance of their *alabados* chanting. Their piety peaked during Lent and Holy Week with private flagellation rituals in the moradas and public processions of the Cross.

Historically, the institutional church seems to have been very nervous about mystical experiences and this kind of popular piety. In the nineteenth century Archbishops Lamy and Salpointe tried to suppress these ascetical practices during the "Americanization" of the Church. They had determined that public rituals of penance and flagellation threatened traditional Catholic orthodoxy. Undeterred, the Brotherhood went underground, becoming a secret society. There was a breakthrough in 1947, when Archbishop Bryne opened a new relationship with the Brotherhood. The then modern American nation, born in the Enlightenment, in asserting the preeminence of Reason, did indeed keep its spiritual experience in the backroom closet. Perhaps because of this obscurity, a deep fascination with all manifestations of popular spirituality developed among anthropologists, sociologists, novelists and other intellectuals.

Today at Santuario del Chimayo I could sense the powerful presence of the Brotherhood and its continuing influence in villages of the Upper Grand Valley. The presence is evident both in the palpable social sphere and also in the intangible but cohesive spirit of the region. In the journal *The North American Geographer*, Jeffrey S. Smith writes:

---

4. Weigle, *Brothers of Light*, 51.

> Not only have the Penitentes been the spiritual leaders of the community, but throughout the year they have provided services that might otherwise have gone undone. They have cared for the sick and poor, interred the deceased, organized wakes and rosaries at funerals, assisted the widowed, and administered the law and order within the village.[5]

Note that from the early history of the Church, we know that these activities precisely describe the ministry of the Order of Deacons.

Alberto Lopez Pulido offers a deeper understanding of the Brotherhood in his book *The Sacred World of the Penitentes*. He brings the reader to the inner heart of this spirituality, which includes care for those in need, prayer and meditation, and modeling Christ-like behavior. Pulido shares the personal stories of members of the Brotherhood, whose families go back many generations. Pulido contends that writers and historians, in their insensitivity to things spiritual, have undermined the primary place that the Penitentes have had in popular piety. As he shares personal testimonies from members, his book reveals the passionate Christian spirituality which imbues their rituals.

But going back to 1936 and Carl N. Taylor's "Agony in Mexico," we find an example of a negative narrative. He witnessed the brotherly solidarity of this spiritual movement within the life of the Hispano pueblos in the area, but he was upset by the flagellation and crucifixion rituals. This reinforced Euro-American negative stereotypes of the Penitentes.

The "canary in the gold mine," is a metaphor coming from the California goldfields that relates to social injustice. The miners of 1849, as they dug tunnels deep into the Sierra Nevada, carried little bamboo cages holding live yellow canaries. The damp interiors of the mine tunnels often emanated poisonous gases and the sensitive little bird in the cage was a first sign of danger. Dead canary: run for your life! In the prophetic tradition of the Jewish scriptures, how the community cares for the widow, orphan and sojourner was the "canary in the gold mine" for the People of God. Oppression of the poor and vulnerable would bring God's punitive judgment. The Brotherhood of the Penitents inherits this Biblical consciousness in its attentive care for those in need in the community. To "act in charity" is a core value for the Brotherhood.

---

5. Smith, "Los Hermanos Penitentes," 73.

North of Santa Fe, New Mexico — The Penitentes

Walk with me as we follow a procession on Good Friday evening, moving slowly on the city sidewalk in downtown Santa Ana, California. We wait at the signal for dense homebound traffic to stop and we follow the direction of the police officers as we cross the street. Latino mothers, wearing dark headscarves, gather little children hand-in-hand as a nurturing mother hen gathers her chicks. An hour ago there was a sudden rain shower but the sky is clear now, wispy steam rises from the street. Thunder in the distance is the last remnant from the departing spring storm.

As you gaze ahead to the start of the long procession, you see a long-haired man bent over, carrying a huge, heavy wooden cross. The crowd begins to sing, "Perdona tu pueblo Señor"—"Forgive your people, Lord." The procession stops at the front door of the University of California Clinic. A short step ladder is set up. A woman climbs with assistance and begins to read one of the Stations of the Cross. At the end of the mediation she offers her own prayer: for those incarcerated at the Orange County Jail nearby and for her own son, who has been there for the past month.

The Procession of the Cross, Via Crucis, proceeds, winding through the busy streets, singing penitential songs on this Good Friday night, praying the fourteen Stations of the Cross. Men and women alternate, carrying the heavy burden of this cross.

As you imagine this scene, how do you think it would be received if it were passing through the main street of your home town today? Surprisingly, as the procession carefully walks through the dense streets of downtown, families out shopping or going to dinner, pull aside from the sidewalk, and reverence the procession by removing hats and making the Sign of the Cross. This Good Friday procession with a large, heavy cross reminds these Latinos of their hometown pueblos, where the same procession could be happening on this night. Some of these observers interrupt their evening plans and join the procession as it winds its way back to the parish church.

In this Via Crucis, participants walk with Jesus in his Passion towards the Cross and Crucifixion. This was a spiritual practice spread throughout the Western world by the Franciscans.

In a previous chapter on El Sanctuario del Chimayo, I share the moving experience my wife Janice had with our son Erik at the Shrine of the Healing Sand. El Sanctuario at that time had the sacramental part-time presence only of a very old priest. However, one layman was the guardian of the Shrine. It was he, who with tender compassion, guided our son to stand within the sacred hole from which the healing sand is taken. He laid his hands on Erik's shoulders and prayed for him. The pastoral, deaconal charism of that man convinces me that he was a member of the Penitentes Brethren.

14.

Monument Valley, Utah
—Eclipse of the Moon

> An eclipse is caused by the death of the orb, which is revived by the immortal bearers of the sun and moon. During an eclipse of the moon, the family is awakened to await its recovery. Similarly, a journey is interrupted and work ceases during an eclipse of the sun. Songs referring to the Hozhoji, or rite of blessing, are chanted by anyone knowing them, otherwise the passing of an eclipse is awaited in silence. It is not considered auspicious to have a ceremony in progress during an eclipse of the sun or moon, and a ceremony is often deferred on this account. The rising generation, however, pays little or no attention to this custom.
>
> —Trudy Griffen-Pierce[1]

A WARM JUNIPER-SCENTED BREEZE caresses Janice and Erik and me as we sit on an ancient wooden bench under a sheltering ramada on a rocky bluff overlooking the iconic mesas of Monument Valley, Utah. We are in front of the historic Goulding's Trading Post. A few feet behind us are the fragile remains of a rude, rustic adobe cabin where the man himself, John Wayne, spent his nights during the filming of John Ford's movies: *Stagecoach* (1939), *Fort Apache* (1948), *She Wore a Yellow Ribbon* (1949), and *The Searchers* (1956).

The Almanac promises that the moon will rise this evening at seven and its eclipse begins forty-five minutes after. I love the colors of the Western horizon after sunset: the reds, oranges and purples. For a few minutes—less than ten, a couple of the famous mesas change from cinnabar-vermillion

---

1. Griffen-Pierce, *Earth Is My Mother*, 41.

to a luminous gold, then quickly fade to reddish-brown, becoming dark shadows in the desert dusk.

There's the moon rising as promised! Strange to look around and see, in the Goulding's Resort with all the rooms full, near the end of peak season, that we are alone. No one else is around. A slight shadow appears on the left edge of the moon and the magic begins. Eclipse. We have perfect seats for a rare celestial show. The eclipse unfolds slowly, but after forty-five minutes the moon is completely covered and then the conclusion: we are expecting a dark disc, instead the circular plane begins to glow red. Amber lights emanate from the darkened circle. Surrealistic. And we are quite alone.

The next day, as I pay for some postcards at the park office, I ask the Navajo/Diné receptionist: "Did you see the eclipse? It was beautiful." Not making eye-contact, she responds softly,

"We try to avoid doing that."

An hour later, the family meets our Diné guide, Harry Nez, who is taking us to remote Mystery Valley and a long haul on deep, sandy roads in his GMC four-wheel-drive. We are going to be exploring Anasazi ruins and pristine petroglyph rock art. I ask Harry about the Diné traditions concerning a lunar eclipse.

Monument Valley, Utah—Eclipse of the Moon

Lunar eclipse at Monument Valley, Utah. 2015. Photo by author.

"The moon is sacred to the Diné and you don't stare at the moon," he says, "It will affect your body. A pregnant woman is especially in danger. The way the sun and moon and earth line up is a time that is special, sacred. We need to show reverence. My family doesn't eat or drink during this time; we stay inside our hogan."

Harry expertly weaves through sagebrush and creosote, gingerly maintaining his speed so that we are not caught in the precarious shifting sand. Erik loves the dramatic lurching of the car, but I am hoping I don't throw up.

In the journal, *Indian Country*, Navajo cultural specialist Rudy Begay shares more information about the Diné respect for the spiritual power of the lunar eclipse:

> If a pregnant woman sees an eclipse of any kind, be it solar or lunar, it might affect the mind of the woman or also in the future it will affect the health of a baby, requiring a special ceremony for purification.[2]

And Navajo ethnobotanist Arnold Clifford reveals:

> The stars are not just there. There's a purpose for them out there. They're very powerful. It's a place of death out there. It's a place we don't really want to talk about, out there. It's a place that we're supposed to avoid. It's a place reserved for the holy people, for specific types of holy people.[3]

We finally arrive in a sheltered canyon. A huge overhang of rock creates the illusion of the apse of a great Gothic cathedral. High above us, an eroded circle in the overhanging rock presents an ancient arch. We sit in the sand beside an Anasazi ruin. Harry takes something from his car and carefully unwraps it—a Navajo flute. He surprises us with a haunting, ancient melody that echoes in the canyon.

After several hours visiting Mystery Valley, we travel on a firm, dirt road to the nearby paved highway.

In the silence of our last minutes with Harry Nez, I had these thoughts about the moon: the Euro-American mind may discount these taboos of the Diné during a lunar eclipse. Nevertheless, we know the moon has power. Janice, Erik and I live near the Pacific Ocean and it is very evident

2. Begay, "Avert Your Eyes."
3. Begay, "Avert Your Eyes."

how the pull of the moon brings about the tides. Janice, with her forty-five years at Mission Hospital, Laguna Beach, California, can tell plenty of stories about the increase in births during a full moon. The emergency room and the obstetrics unit where she worked became crazy with odd and peculiar cases, intense activity, and an increase in psychiatric admissions during a full moon.

A month after our Monument Valley journey, I am walking with our son Erik in the hills surrounding our home in Laguna Niguel, California. A large, orange, November full-moon looms right in front of us. "Where is the moon? I ask Erik.

"Over there!" He says. He keeps his attention on the moon as we walk our mile-long circular route and begin to climb the hill heading home. Because we walk in a circle, the position of the moon relative to us changes.

"Where is the moon now?" I ask Erik.

"Over there!"

"Did you move the moon with your finger?" He holds his index finger up to the moon and moves the finger sidewise. Mentally four years old, he has not lost his sense of enchantment and wonder.

"You are moving the moon, Erik!"

"I like it!" he laughs.

15.

Navajo Nation, Four Corners —Earth Medicine

> Medical treatment is older than intelligence in man. The dog hunts the fields for his special grass medicine; the bear dresses the wound of her cub or fellow-bear with perhaps as much intelligence as primitive man observes in his empirical practice. Primitive man does not know why his medicine cures; he simply knows that it does cure.
>
> —Matilda Croxe Stevenson[1]

OLD NEW MEXICO HIGHWAY 666 (now U.S. Route 491) branches off Interstate 40 and heads north from Gallup, through desolate, wind-carved red sandstone canyons towards the Navajo and Hopi people. Clusters of white crosses pop up at each tight turn—these are roadside memorials marking violent auto deaths, many due to drunk-driving.

I had heard about the Indian Swap Meet and our family put it on our bucket-list during our RV camping trip in New Mexico. I searched for the right highway and did not have to look for long as I could see a line of cars parked on the road which gave the location away. Across the street, bales of hay were sold from flatbeds directly into waiting pickup trucks. Small corrals displayed sheep, goats, and saddled horses for sale.

We followed the Navajo, Zuni and Hopi families as they moved towards three long aisles of tables and booths which we would walk for almost two miles. This was a family affair: Grandmothers in traditional, long red-and-blue velvet dresses with heavy "old pawn" bracelets and necklaces,

---

1. Stevenson, *Ethnobotany of the Zuni Indians*, 39.

were holding onto grandchildren as parents browsed through heaping piles of auto parts, computer drives and accessories, and fresh fruit and vegetables.

I am in a philosophic mood this morning as we begin to wander among the aisles of abundance. Of course, visiting with and learning from the people who have kept alive the complex family and spiritual and cultural traditions in this corner of the world, and who happily have found ways of informing, if not integrating, what has gone before with the present dominant Anglo-American ways of doing things—this has made me acutely aware of what that dominant culture, my rationalistic, "buffered-self" culture, has set aside; how it has perversely deprived itself of its birthright. I think of the humbling insight of a great thinker of the twentieth century:

> Out of sheer envy we are obliged to smile at the Indians' naiveté and to plume ourselves on our cleverness; for otherwise we would discover how impoverished and down at the heels we are. Knowledge does not enrich us; it removes us more and more from the mythic world in which we were once at home by right of birth.[2]

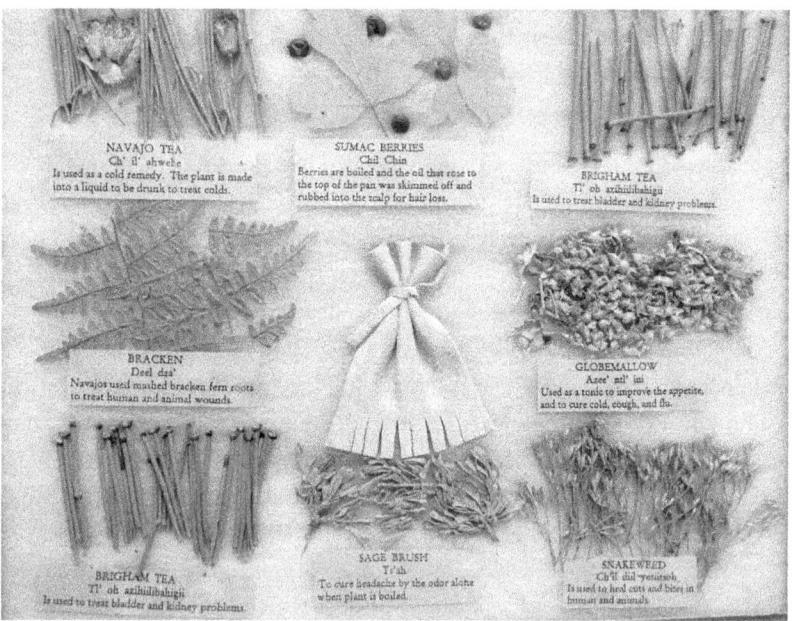

Diné herbal sampler. Author's collection.

2. Jung, *Memories, Dreams, Reflections*, 252.

Navajo Nation, Four Corners—Earth Medicine

And I wonder where the depletion started—and why. Aristotle? The Scholastic Philosophers? The Enlightenment? Surely the scientific approach, rationalism, in the past lived and thrived alongside the world of the stories of the archetypes, intuition and folk-learned spirituality. Socrates knew his Homer, Hildegard knew her Boethius and even Voltaire was intrigued by the ghost of Hamlet's father. When did we occidentals become so one-dimensional? Surely the medieval German abbess, who, though living in a grimmer, unkinder time, still has something to teach us—something that the denizens of the Indian Swap Meet appear never to have unlearned.

> Bramble leaves *(Rubus fruticosus)*: The bramble, on which blackberries grow, is warm rather than cold. If anyone suffers a disorder of the lungs, and has a cough from his chest, let him take root of sneezewort, bramble leaves, hyssop and a little origanum, add honey, and boil it all in good wine, then strain it through a cloth, drink sufficient quantity of it after a good meal, and do this often, and his lungs will be restored to healthy.[3]

This is an amazing place. Small booths with tables of hand-made jewelry with real turquoise—not the reconstituted powder mixed with plastic that is found in the tourist shops. An aromatic cloud hints of mutton stew and homemade lamb sausages. Fry-bread made to order or filled with lamb and beans as the Navajo Taco. Recordings of singing and drumming from Indian ceremonies are playing. Handmade Navajo dolls, including a striking tableau of a Navajo woman kneeling at a loom with a half-finished rug.

Then I saw the table covered with small sacks of healing herbs: The Navajo Spiritual Pharmacy. One bag had a bold label which read:

Evil Way Medicine: Cold, Nightmares, Ghost-Chasing Ceremony.

I picked up the bag but hesitated to ask how its contents might be used. The Navajo lady who sat behind the table looked at me as if to say, "You don't know what you are dealing with." Next to this item were tiny bags of fine, yellow corn pollen: pure, concentrated spiritual energy. I bought both the Evil Way Medicine and some corn pollen to remind my world-religions class how close we are to another world, if we care to look.

---

3. Strehlow, *Hildegard of Bingen's Medicine*, 69.

Author at Hitali/Medicine Man Hogan, Gallup, New Mexico. 2015. Photo by Janice Karelius.

During our four-week visit to sites within the Navajo reservation, I had some enlightening exchanges with several people of that tribe about origins and customs and spirituality. But when I asked about the specific use of various herbs in healing ceremonies, the responses became vague and oblique. This nation does not advertise its pharmacopeia; it does not lay out what it knows in a Physician's Desk Reference. Only the few Navajo who had gone through extensive training under a medicine person—a contemporary *nesjaja hatali*, perhaps—would have this information. Sacred knowledge is diluted in power when too many people are in the know.

As we traveled through the reservation lands throughout the Four Corners, we gazed in wonder at the vast red-sand landscape. Here the weather can be harsh and can change suddenly. On one trip from Santa Fe to Gallup, we saw a car blown off Interstate 40 and even a freight train that had been derailed by powerful winds. We might awake one morning to dress in shorts and T-shirts, but after lunch, crossing the Continental Divide near Gallup, slushy snow covers our windshield. Parched, arid land is suddenly drenched by monsoonal rains, dry washes where we hiked yesterday and kicked up dust, are now gushing in violent flash-flood. The powerful arcs of Nature seem to track the bizarre swings between the old ways and the new which pervade the Navajo lands. Elders lament the loss of traditional ways, as Diné youth dress as gangster-wannabes with their brightly colored Nike shoes and designer sunshades.

Despite the incongruities, traditions do continue—including the gathering of wild plants for medicine and ceremonies. The Diné spiritual world centers on the bonds between living and inanimate things. Plants are not picked wholesale or indiscriminately, but for a specific purpose. For example, if sage is needed for healing for cold or flu, the herbalist offers a prayer to the plant expressing why it is needed and an offering of a pinch of corn pollen may be sprinkled over the plant.

This indigenous desert world is fragile and unstable, in constant process of deconstruction. Dark forces of witches and (to the outsider, mysterious) skinwalkers lurk in the shadows. (The bundle of medicine I purchased at the swap meet cures curses pronounced by skinwalkers and witches, though I do not profess to have any insight as to their correct use).

It is the *hatali*, the healer, the medicine-man or medicine-woman who has the power to restore harmony, balance, *hozhó* (beauty). Through hand-trembling, incised rocks or crystals, the hatali will diagnose the cause of an illness. "Dis-ease" always has a spiritual cause: perhaps the violation of a taboo, such as contact with a protected animal or a dead person. Healing chants can be short, lasting just a few hours, or they may take several days to complete. Navajo soldiers who left for military service in Iraq and Afghanistan received a Blessing Way Ceremony because they would be beyond the protective enclosure of the Four Sacred Mountains. And soldiers who returned from war with post-traumatic stress disorder needed the hatali to perform an Enemy Way Ceremony, as a kind of exorcism of the pollution of evil in the body and to restore hozhó.

There are about sixty Diné healing ceremonies, many of which last for four days or more. The hatali must conduct the rituals precisely and in this he or she is helped by the constant attention of family members. A healthy person is one whose being is a congruence of mind, body and spirit, and in ceremony the healer seeks to elicit balance and harmony against a backdrop of dark forces, which can cause sickness through pollution. All animate and inanimate entities are spirit presences that can help or harm us in our journey toward wholeness.

Herbal medicine is at the heart of this process of healing and harmony. One example, sage, is a common and powerful herbal aid. It grows almost everywhere. It protects against evil spirits, is often used in exorcisms and in daily protective purification. Sage is seen as a cure for colon and stomach disorders, sinus infections, colds and fever. Medicine men and women carry medicine bundles. The contents of each are unique and personal. They may hold healing stones and crystals, fetishes and corn-pollen and pipes, whose sacred smoke carries prayers to the spirits.

Until recently, traditional medicine was the only healing help available to Diné. Nowadays, if you visit the Navajo Health Center in Window Rock, Arizona, you will see that the concept of spiritual harmony is deeply embedded within the modern concrete walls which house all the modern medical equipment and Western training. Each tradition can inform the other. In line with this, I came across a very interesting article by P.J. Johnston, "Psychiatric Drugs and Healing."

> My university requires its medical and psychological students to take courses on ethno-medicine and medical pluralism so that these future practitioners of Western biomedicine will cooperate with rather than counterproductively fight against the health goals of their patients from other cultural backgrounds. The Religion and Medicine class I mentioned before was designed to allow students to meet this requirement. The university hospitals routinely ask you what herbal or nontraditional treatments you may be pursuing along with your conventional medical treatment when they ask you what medicines you are taking, hoping to minimize destructive medical conflicts. A classic example of a case where physician rigidity led to a wholesale breakdown in treatment is Anne Fadiman's "The Spirit Catches You and You Fall Down," about a Hmong patient treated for epilepsy by doctors who could not or would not accommodate Hmong medical goals, to tragic effects.[4]

I have created a fictional person who is a composite of several Navajo herbal healers that I have known. She is called Kai (Willow Tree) Totsonnie, of the Big Water Clan. She is six feet tall in her bright orange Nike shoes. Luminescent black hair flows down her back to her leather belt. Her height and large hands remind me she was a member of the 2004 Ganado High School Girls' Basketball team that won the Arizona State championship. We follow her as she walks with intentional care through sagebrush and mesquite looking for the earth medicine. She tells us how her grandmother tutored her for ten years in the ways of healing with herbs and prayer.

---

4. Johnston, "Psychiatric Drugs and Healing."

"This is my church," she declares, gesturing to the expanse of rocky desert, a sea of sagebrush, juniper and mesquite. "I feel closest to God walking here; it is filled with spirit presences. The sound of the wind in the cottonwoods, animal voices and even a pile of rocks, they speak to me. My grandmother taught me to be silent, still, listen, and watch for signs. The shape and color of a plant can tell of how it cures. A plant that looks like a worm could cure worms. The Hopi look for weasel plants: because the weasel can dig rapidly through the sandy earth, the plant could help childbirth progress faster. I gather plants that can help with a particular cure and dry them in my grandmother's hogan. When I need to use them, I make a tea by boiling leaves from the plant."

Alice Henkel published the guide, *Wild Medicinal Herbs of the United States*, in 1906. She goes into detail about the preparation of herbal medicines. Annual plants have their roots dug up in April/May; perennial herbs are harvested in October/November. At these times the medicinal properties of the plants are most potent. The plants are washed or shaken, they can be hung from rafters out of the sun to dry for later use or they can be used right away.

Kai has much to add to the mechanics of herb-gathering. She looks off into the distance as if uttering a holy warning. "We don't come into the place without spiritual preparation. Your mind must be in a pure place with good thoughts and intentions. I have Euro-Americans asking me all of the time what herbs they could take to have better health. It is a kind of spiritual hedonism that upsets me and makes me want to be silent and not respond. Our sacred traditions and our communion with Mother Earth are not another convenient tool for those obsessed with health."

We walk around cholla cactus which leans toward us, trying to snag our clothes. The sagebrush and creosote are wet from last night's rain and emit pungent perfume. I sheepishly pull out a colorful folder: *A Pocket Naturalist Guide to Medicinal Plants*. Vivid photographs of plants with their descriptions, habitats and the diseases for which they are the remedy. I show it to Kai, expecting to be chastised. "Yes, I've seen that," she says with a quick glance. "Okay if it helps you, but remember what I said about entering your exploration with right mind, heart and spirit as you walk among our spiritual kin."

Our time together is drawing to a close. The crimson cliffs around us darken as the sun sets behind the White Mountains. This transition between day and night is when dark spirits and witches lurk in shadows, seeking the weak and vulnerable. Shrieking sage hens suddenly leap into the air from dense salt brush. The face of a coyote peers between the brush and disappears. A few minutes later, I see a small, brown-skinned, shirtless man running away into a dry wash. "Skinwalker," Kai sighs. I hear humming, soft singing. Her lips move in quiet prayer.

I want mindfully to learn more about these desert plants through which I have marched in the past, focusing on some distant goal, stomping forth unconsciously through the dense brush. This landscape is alive with healing and blessing. These are not dry, useless weeds, but living gifts implanted by God for healing and harmony.

16.

Mesa Verde, Colorado
—The Kiva as Sacred Ground

> We need to become aware of what might be called "a longer narrative" in which "the others" who have been made absent by those who control public or institutional histories are now being restored as people who are fully present. They are no longer a presumed and distant "them" removed from a vague and tacit "us."
> —Phillip Sheldrake[1]

COV DAVIS HELD THE hand of her three-year-old son, as she balanced the weight of her two-year-old daughter on her hip, swaying slightly to calm the restless young one. Her beaded moccasins crunched coarse, dry sand as she gazed at the hole that was the entrance to the Hopi kiva at Walpi Mesa, in northern Arizona. Standing here on this mesa seemed like being on a spaceship hovering over the Earth. The hazy October sun set behind the San Francisco Peaks to the west; rain poured out of a purple-hued thundercloud to the south. Jagged lightning flashed towards the world below and the shockwave of thunder frightened the children and they clung to their mother for protection. Cov sensed an invisible barrier between herself and the kiva, knowing this sacred space was reserved only for the private ceremonies of the Eagle Clan.

But this night was a special night. Her husband, Father John Davis, an Episcopal priest who had ministered to the Navajo and Hopi for the past twelve years, was leaving the reservation for a new assignment in California.

---

1. Sheldrake, *Spaces for the Sacred*, 21.

As night descended upon the mesa she could see more clearly the luminous glow coming from the entrance of the kiva.

"Come over here . . . " Father John whispered to Cov as he emerged from the kiva, still perched on the rungs of the ladder that led down through the entrance.

"Are you sure this is okay? I don't think the children will be quiet, and they will disrupt whatever is going on down there."

"It's okay," Father John responded. "Remember that the Hopi have a special reverence for children. Tonight they are the special guests."

Many years later, Cov would recall what happened next. With John's help she conveyed the children down the sturdy cottonwood ladder into the kiva. A small fire of pinyon pine was burning in a corner, and by means of some ancient engineering the smoke went out somewhere so it was not bothersome. Benches carved into the sides of the earthen hole were filled with men from the village. Some of their faces reflected deeply altered states. Others looked to Cov in greeting, there were slight smiles, and nods. No one was speaking; any sound was greatly amplified in the enclosed space. As Cov looked around at the men seated there, memories of what connected her to each person flickered through her mind. Such precious friends! She ached with fondness, love even, and the beginnings of grief.

Kiva ladder, Mesa Verde, Colorado. 2015. Photo by author.

Mesa Verde, Colorado—The Kiva as Sacred Ground

Thunder still boomed in the distance. Three of the men began to beat a drum in an alternating cadence. The rhythm was met by a low, throaty humming. The humming became the words of chants and the sound enfolded Cov and the children. She looked at the faces of her son and daughter, worried again that they might begin to fret and cry. But the soft rhythm of the drumming and chanting filled the space to join the hint of spicy pinyon smoke and the eyes of the children widened in enchantment and wonder.

As Cov looks back on that last night on Walpi Mesa she is sure her family was in the kiva for several hours, and for the entire time the children were in an enchanted state. The family left the kiva and the reservation with blessings from the people to carry them west to Orange County, California.

Mable Dodge Luhan, in *Edge of Taos Desert*, shares another story of a kiva experience.

There was a white man who was brought into the tribal community because the Indians were fond of him to such an extent that he was allowed to attend their ceremonies so long as he was blindfolded. He remembers that once he was taken down into the kiva ceremonial space.

> It was a round, underground chamber with a roof made of seven portions, by tree trunks joined and fitted together, with heavy dirt on the top. In the center of this roof, a round opening to the sky, and below it, resting on the earth, lay a great round stone. There was a stout thong made of hide tied about the stone with its end lying on the ground. The Indians sat in a circle on their haunches, their backs against the earthen wall.[2]

They again blindfolded him and, as he sat, he could hear a low chanting, repeated phrases like a mantra. This went on for a while and without his sight, his other senses were heightened. The hypnotic humming continued and,

> at regular intervals a wind passed against his cheeks as though the air was suddenly displaced before him. Round and round him something moved, each time faster while the humming sound grew higher in pitch. Something rose on the solid body of the chant. . .rose in the room, fanning him briskly, higher and higher until he no longer felt the air moving on his face and it stirred his hair no more, but the great whine of an enormous rotary motor filled the hollow chamber of earth above him. For a few seconds

---

2. Luhan, *Edge of Taos Desert*, 4.

Desert Spirit Places

only, and then, apparently, it passed out through the roof and soared away.[3]

The sound went off into the night air and faded away. The humming and chanting continued in the kiva, and then the man could hear the greater sound returning, hovering over the kiva and then entering the kiva chamber again.

> Once more he felt the air stir across his face as the thing passed and re-passed him. It slowed down and its whine, too, sank to a low, deep sound. It came to rest in the center, and the men stopped chanting and began talking in Indian.[4]

They removed the blindfold from the man, he looked around, and everything in the kiva looked as it was when he first entered.

October 2014. Jan, Erik and I are walking along a winding paved road from a parking lot at Mesa Verde National Park down steep inclines toward Spruce Tree House. Residual raindrops from a passing thunderstorm drip on us from juniper and pinyon pine. At a wide turn on the path, we pause to view a huge rocky alcove within which are set the ruins of a Pueblo village which had been occupied between CE 1200 and 1280. We continue walking towards the sound of a waterfall and find the ancient seep-water source which sustained the settlement in this desert mountain terrain.

We approach close enough to touch the walls of the impressive ruins. Two kiva courtyards spread out to the left and right, each with a ladder inviting visits to reconstructions of kiva sacred space. As the early inhabitants once did, I climb down a cottonwood ladder and step over to the walls with their recesses and stone furnishings.

Using a National Park Service booklet for orientation, I can see above me, cribbed wooden roof beams supported by six pillars or pilasters. Traditionally, at the center of the kiva is a fire pit with a stone heat-deflector next to it. I can see a ventilator opening in the wall and something that looks like a chimney that must have pulled in outside air. The smoke from the fire would have escaped up through the entrance hole. And there in the floor is a small circular hole, the *sipapu*, believed by many Pueblo people to be a portal to the world from whence they came. There are niches in the kiva

---

3. Luhan, *Edge of Taos Desert*, 4–5.
4. Luhan, *Edge of Taos Desert*, 4–5.

walls where ceremonial masks and sacred corn could be stored, and there is a special space for an altar.

I sit on one of the recessed stone benches. My mind flits back to what Cov told me about her visit to the Hopi kiva with her children. It is late afternoon, near closing time at the Park. I am alone. Jan and Erik wait for me in the ruins above. Soft orange beams of sunlight shine down the ladder entrance hole. This is not so much an historic ruin as ancient holy ground: a well-prayed-in place. The prayer people who lived here died a thousand years ago, but Pueblo people today would honor their presence.

I contemplate the three narratives I have shared with you. One is a memory from an Anglo woman who had a powerful experience as a spiritual guest with her family in the Walpi Hopi kiva. One is a story told by Mabel Luhan, a transplanted Eastern artist, who became enchanted with the people at Taos Pueblo. Her narrative sounds like a sensational event to add to a collection of spiritual experiences. The third narrative comes from the National Park Service, technical information gleaned from archaeologists to help the visitor understand the physical layout of the kiva.

But above all, this is still holy ground, mysterious space where the ancient ones communed with the Holy.

Kiva interior, Spruce Tree House, Mesa Verde, Colorado. 2014. Photo by author.

Phillip Sheldrake reminds us:

Desert Spirit Places

> Narrative is critical to our identity, for we all need a story to live by in order to make sense of the otherwise unrelated events of life and to find a sense of dignity. It is only by enabling alternative stories to be heard that an elitist "history" may be pried open to offer an entry point for the oppressed who have otherwise been excluded from the history of public places.[5]

Whose narrative is being told in this place? Anecdotes from Anglo friends, anthropologists, government caretakers, or vestiges of the people who once lived here? French Philosopher Paul Ricoeur contends that the narrative of this holy ground kiva includes history but also "fiction," what we may call "myths," because in traditional cultures, myth is actualized story.

Here is a narrative of the ancient ones who once lived here and who encountered the sacred in this kiva. The Creator made the First World. Spider Woman and Sotuknang instructed the people to honor with gratitude the Creator. Fire laid waste this First World, because the people forgot the Creator. However, there was a remnant of the people who did remember the Creator and they went underground to seek refuge with the Ant People. In time, the Creator permitted the people to come up from the underworld into a beautiful New World. But the connection between the animals and the people had been lost and again the people forgot the Creator. Then ice and snow destroyed the New World. There was another cycle of reemergence and the creation of a Third World, and again the people forgot the Creator and that world was destroyed by flood. Finally, the gods guided the people to emerge into a recreated Fourth World. The kiva represents the memory of this narrative with the sipapu, the portal through which the ancestors entered and re-entered the four worlds.

To what narrative have you given your heart? Sitting in quiet contemplation in the kiva, standing in the desert as morning light breaks out of Monument Valley to the east, kneeling before the Blessed Sacrament at my parish, I embrace the narrative of my life, which includes remembering the Creator in gratitude for all the gifts and graces in those times when I was at the end of my resources and running on empty. Being in sacred space evokes deep gratitude within me.

---

5. Sheldrake, *Spaces for the Sacred*, 19.

17.

Antelope Valley, California —Seeing the Divine Within

In the fourth century AD the deserts of Egypt, Palestine, Arabia and Persia were peopled by a race of men... They sought a way to God that was uncharted and freely chosen, not inherited from others who had mapped it out beforehand. They sought a God whom they alone could find, not one who was "given" in a set or stereotyped from somebody else.
—Thomas Merton[1]

To be shaken out of the ruts of ordinary perception, to be shown for a few timeless hours the outer and inner world, not as they appear to an animal obsessed with survival or to a human being obsessed with words and notions, but as they are apprehended directly and unconditionally, by Mind at Large—this is an experience of inestimable value to everyone and especially to the intellectual.
—Aldous Huxley[2]

I AM WALKING ON a coyote track through a vast sea of creosote bushes in the Mojave Desert, about twenty miles east of Palmdale California. It is a mild winter day, the gentle wind dances the spindly branches in all directions. Protecting my face from a sudden swat of a wildly moving branch, I try to see the way ahead on the faint trail. The problem with creosote is that the plants are about as high as a regular human, so visibility ahead and perspective of the landscape are obscured. However, I march on, winding

1. Merton, *Wisdom of the Desert*, 3.
2. Huxley, *Doors of Perception*, 173.

through the dense foliage. Suddenly, rock walls and a carefully constructed rock cylinder that looks like a well-head appear before me. I have come upon ruins in the desert. There is plenty here to intrigue me: extensive foundations of buildings, animal corrals—but where am I?

Later I find out that this is what is left of Llano del Rio, founded a hundred years ago by one Job Harriman. He created a desert colony, an attempt at building a self-sustaining community run along quasi-socialist lines. At its peak there were about one thousand residents here, raising grains, rabbits, peanuts and alfalfa. However, the brief blush of vitality ended when an earthquake fault drained away the main source of water. Less than four years after its inception, the colony moved to Louisiana.

A generation later, Aldous Huxley (1894–1963), famous as the author of *Brave New World*, came to this desert place to live for eight years with his wife Maria and son Matthew. Huxley, a lifelong seeker of inner- and outer-mystical experiences, found a spiritual home here for a while, fed by the silence and encounters with animate and inanimate nature. Obviously, the desert sparked immense creativity within Huxley: he wrote eight books, several screenplays and many essays in this desert place.

What did Huxley experience in this vast expanse of sand, sagebrush and creosote? He shares this reflection:

> But the light forgives, the distances forget, and this great crystal of silence whose base is as large as Europe and whose height, for all practical purposes, is infinite, can coexist with things of a far higher order of discrepancy than canned sentiment or vicarious sport. Jet planes, for example—the stillness is so massive that it can absorb even jet planes. The screaming rash mounts to its intolerable climax and fades again, mounts as another of the monsters rips through the air, and once more diminishes and is gone. But even at the height of the outrage the mind can still remain aware of that which surrounds it, that which preceded and will outlast it.[3]

---

3. Huxley, "Double Crisis."

Aldous Huxley. *Life Magazine*, January 11, 1954.

Although a professed agnostic, Huxley encountered Something Infinite in the desert vastness and silence. This desert experience sparked deeper searches for communion with this Presence. An earlier experience with peyote in 1930 with Aleister Crowley would lead to serious, guided journeys with mescaline (the key ingredient in peyote) in 1953, and LSD in 1955, with psychiatrist Humphrey Osmond.

Cultural journalist Steffie Nelson contends that Huxley's move to America and his desert experiences fostered his enchantment with the mind-altering pharmacopeia, mysticism and spiritual enlightenment.

> . . . without the dedicated and well-documented cosmic explorations of Aldous Huxley and his cohorts, [the decade of the Sixties] would have looked very different. It's not an exaggeration to say that, without Huxley, Timothy Leary might never have tuned in and turned on, and Jim Morrison might never have broken on through.[4]

In the history of religions, entheogens have been a common gateway to communion with the Holy, augmented by vision quests, yoga, prayer and meditation. Entheogens are any psychoactive drug or plant substance used for spiritual experience. Previously, "hallucinogen" and "psychedelic" were terms for these substances, but those words have connections to psychiatric

4. Nelson, "Aldous Huxley's Brave New World."

pathology, so entheogen is now the accepted academic term. In contrast to the modern world of private spiritual experience, the entheogens of traditional cultures were taken and shared within a community context. There were rituals of purification and preparation, and there was guidance from an experienced shaman or spiritual master who walked the participant through the inner journey, a journey that might well render a message for the tribal community or initiate a psychic transformation of the spiritual traveler into a shaman. In traditional culture, one did not take entheogens for personal spiritual insight alone; it was always for the common good, the enrichment of the family, clan or tribe. We of the Anglo-American individualist culture live in a very different world.

> In a strict sense, only those vision-producing drugs that can be shown to have figured in shamanic or religious rites would be designated entheogens, but in a looser sense, the term could also be applied to other drugs, both natural and artificial, that induce alterations of consciousness similar to those documented for ritual ingestion of traditional entheogens.[5]

In 1973, in Laguna Beach (once, as it happens, home to the proponent of psychedelics, Timothy Leary), the ambulance arrived at South Coast Medical Center. My wife, Jan, who was on the medical staff, began to treat a young man who, wearing only a football helmet and cowboy boots, had jumped off a cliff onto the sandy beach below. On a bad LSD trip, he thought he could fly and broke both his legs.

A few years later a teenage couple arrived at the emergency room, screaming and thrashing in the ambulance. They had taken jimson weed, a common entheogen consumed by Paiute shamans, and they had come very close to death. Over the years of her medical practice, Jan encountered many spiritual seekers who had taken LSD, peyote, mescaline, mushrooms and other substances. Some lived and some died.

I asked Jan whether she would give us the benefit of her clinical experience in this context, and she offered the following Thoughts from the Emergency Department:

I was employed in the hospital Emergency Department in Laguna Beach as a Registered Nurse and Acute Care / Family Nurse Practitioner, for over forty years, beginning in the late 1960s.

During those early years, among others, Carlos Castaneda published several books for his Doctoral thesis at UCLA, concerning his work as an

5. Ruck et al., "Entheogens."

apprentice in shamanism with a Yaqui Indian shaman. He described, in detail, his mystical experiences and insights while using the psychoactive substances, datura, or jimsonweed, and peyote. He and R. Gordon Wasson, who wrote about psychoactive mushroom use, encouraged the groups in Los Angeles and Orange County seeking spiritual experiences, and enlightenment through mind-altering substances. I arrived in Laguna Beach shortly after Timothy Leary and Richard Alpert (Ram Dass) had left, after making their mark on Laguna Beach culture.

Along with many of my colleagues and friends, I read the books by Castaneda, curious about his descriptions of spirituality obtained through consciousness- expanding substances. We were aware that there was a lot of experimentation with these substances, because of discussions with other friends, and because of a cross-section of patients we saw in the emergency department (ER) under their influence. Unfortunately, our patients experienced none of the wonders Castaneda described. Those who arrived at our door were having what was termed as "a bad trip." They were always wild with fear, completely disoriented, either combative or huddled in corners, shaking and crying. They were difficult to evaluate because of heightened response to physical sensations and their fear that the medical and nursing staff were part of their horrific hallucinations. Medications to calm their intense anxieties were mostly ineffective.

I found, however, that, in an environment of dim lights with soft instrumental music, I might sit quietly and gently enter their world, speaking calmly, guiding the interpretation of some of the hallucinations with imagery that was less frightening. Eventually most patients fell asleep long enough to awaken more calm and unafraid.

The consensus of our ER group was that a trusted guide to maintain the environment, and prevent misinterpretation of inner experiences as frightening, as happened with Castaneda's Yaqui guide, could have limited some need for our interventions. The experimenters would also have incurred fewer physical injuries. I think we would all have agreed with Emmy Savage's evaluation of solitary experimentation.

Emmy Savage, daughter of Charles Savage, MD, a pioneering physician in use of LSD, writes:

> . . . the temptation to experiment with this kind of drug [LSD] is just too great. Lacking the context of a culture that supports

shamanistic guidance for the young, the curious, and the foolish, the possibility for dangerous and even fatal consequences is great. And, regrettably, ours is a culture that is deeply suspicious of the unconscious, of mystery and the spiritual, and resentful of the time it takes for the intimate engagement required for such a therapy to work.[6]

William Johnston, SJ, who has spent most of his life in Japan studying and experiencing Zen Buddhism, shares this observation about entheogens and meditation:

> According to [the Filter Theory of Naranjo], the brain and nervous system are fitted with restrictive filters or barriers of some kind which prevent entrance of such knowledge as man needs for biological survival. These filters are nothing less than a repressive mechanism calculated to impede the inrush of knowledge that would otherwise overwhelm and break us. In this sense they are a sort of protective screen: humankind, unable to bear too much reality, must find some way of blocking things out.
>
> But these protective barriers, this theory continues, can be removed so that more knowledge enters, thus expanding the mind. Probably one way of removing them is by the intake of drugs. Or they are perhaps broken down in certain forms of mental illness. In these cases, the floodgates are opened and reality rushes in, often with horrendous and traumatic consequences. Or again, some people may be born with less restrictive filters; and these are the "psychics" who are open to telepathy, clairvoyance and other parapsychological sources of information. Meditation is also a human and natural way of opening the filters, welcoming the inflow of reality, and expanding the mind. It is a gradual process, a daily practice, in which the filters or barriers are slowly lifted to allow an almost imperceptible inflow of grater reality into the intuitive consciousness—though this unhurried process may, at times, give way to a sudden collapse of barriers that cause massive enlightenment or mystical experience. In all this, meditation is safer than drugs because the meditator, if properly instructed and guided, can integrate the new knowledge and preserve his equilibrium.[7]

In these daunting days of inner spiritual exploration and human consciousness, we have holy help in the time-honored wisdom of the world

6. Savage, "Drug Trials."
7. Johnston, *Silent Music*, 56–57.

spiritualities. At the heart of their heritage of encounters with the Holy are persons foundationally set within a community of faith and the rituals and practices of meditation.

18.

The Dinétah, Arizona-New Mexico —Tony Hillerman: Reading the Signs

A feeling of mystical presence is very real when one looks upon the landscape of the Southwest. A region of scarce water and endless vistas, the Southwest has been a spiritual homeland for countless people, both indigenous and transplanted to the region. And for both these groups, a return to this landscape, be it a daily awakening or a journey's end, is a return home.
—Beverly G. Six[1]

Beyond books and people, nature also points to God and offers signs and wonders indicating God's presence.
—Henri Nouwen[2]

THE DEEP NEVADA NIGHT sky, bejeweled with countless shimmering stars, slowly fades into desert dawn, brightening the crimson-orange eastern horizon. From our viewpoint, hidden behind craggy volcanic rocks, we see a starkly lit military base surrounded by a high fence with razor-wire on top. Through binoculars we see an ambulance and four men in white coats pushing a gurney bearing an almost human form, its thin arms and a greenish head glimmering in the floodlights. An alien creature? The men disappear quickly with the gurney into a grey Quonset hut.

We are watching the science fiction television series the *X-files*. Two FBI agents: Fox Mulder (David Duchovny) and Dana Scully (Gillian

---

1. Six, "Slaying the Monsters," 64.
2. Nouwen, *Discernment*, 53.

Anderson) investigate unsolved paranormal cases. Mulder had an earlier encounter with aliens involving his sister, and he believes that aliens do exist. Scully is the skeptical medical doctor whose assignment at first is to discredit Mulder's theories and his pursuit of the paranormal. As they work together, the conflict changes to trust and eventually into romance, while they discover the U. S. Government's policy of hiding the reality of extra-terrestrial life that has been discovered on earth.

Skeptic meets Believer. Buffered Self meets Porous Self.

Contrasting personalities, where one character is the foil for another in teasing out the story—and the more tortuous the better—is a common motif of detective stories: Sherlock Holmes and John Watson; Nero Wolfe and Archie Goodwin; Bertie Wooster and Jeeves. The motif is so common as to be usual, perhaps archetypal: the divided Self in hot pursuit of hidden truth.

Manisha Aggarwal-Schifellite, in her essay "I Want to Believe," shows that an important influence on Chris Carter, the creator of the *X-files*, was the detective-mystery writer Tony Hillerman, whose mystery stories were set against the backdrop of the desert spirit places of the American Southwest. And that backdrop is a fine place for the rational and the ineffable to find each other.

Aggarwal-Schifellite writes in the online journal, *The Oyster Review*:

> Before the X-Files began in 1993, Joe Leaphorn and Jim Chee solved crimes that couldn't be explained by logic alone in a series of eighteen books by the American Author Tony Hillerman. The two detectives work together and apart on their New Mexico reservation, often clashing with federal agents called in for homicide investigations, or local residents suspicious of police activity.[3]

For many years, in my long solo drives to Nevada to work on archaeological projects, Tony Hillerman has been my guide and companion. At first there were those audio tapes (which often would jam in the tape player), then CDs (half a dozen for each book), and now there are the more accessible Audible.com recordings.

While my students and I would spend a week in my world religions course at Saddleback College in the general study of Native American religion, it was un-numbered hours of driving with Tony Hillerman's desert detectives that brought me into a deeper encounter with tribal spirituality and ceremony. His writing revealed finely defined Southwestern landscapes,

---

3. Aggarwal-Schifellite, "I Want to Believe."

not as decorative backdrops to his intense mystery narratives, but as an integral part, a main character, in what he called "Our Own Holy Land," the Dinétah, the sacred land of the Navajo/Diné.

I felt a kinship with Hillerman in our shared experience of spiritual homecoming as we traveled through this spiritually potent landscape together. In an essay, Hillerman reflects:

> It is an arid landscape, inhospitable, almost empty, with none of the lush green that spells prosperity. It is built far out of human scale, too large for habitation, making man feel tiny, threatened, aware of his fragility and mortality. Perhaps that is why it is good for me—why I seem to need it, and return at every excuse.[4]

There is a "meant-to-be-ness" here; the desert is Hillerman's spiritual home. He was born in the small town of Sacred Heart, Oklahoma, which had been founded as a Benedictine mission to the Pottawatomie people. Son of a rural shopkeeper, he was the only boy at a Roman Catholic school for Indian girls. His early immersion in tribal culture sparked an intuitive awareness of the Other: his Indian classmates within Anglo culture, and his isolation as an Anglo in Indian culture. Returning from World War II, a decorated veteran, he witnessed a Native American cleansing ceremony for marines coming home from the war. A renewed interest in Indian culture complemented his attraction to its values, in its caring for the family and reaction against post-war materialism in America. Hillerman went to work as a journalist in New Mexico and Texas where his beat often covered naked violence and murder. Later, as a journalism instructor at the University of New Mexico, he began to write his mystery novels.

---

4. Hillerman, "Our Own Holy Land," 83.

The Dinétah, Arizona-New Mexico — Tony Hillerman

Author with Erik Karelius at Tony Hillerman's inspiration bench at Rio Grande River, Albuquerque, New Mexico. 2014. Photo by Janice Karelius.

Writers search for a focus that connects what is combusting within themselves and what they experience in the outer world. The key inspiration for Hillerman's focus on murder mysteries within indigenous tribal culture was the Australian author Arthur W. Upfield. The hero of his stories, a half-Australian Aborigine and half-European named Bony Bonaparte, solved crimes using his knowledge of and respect for tribal traditions.

Hillerman reflects:

> When my own Jim Chee of the Navajo Tribal Police unravels a mystery because he understands the ways of his people, when he reads the signs in the sandy bottom of a reservation arroyo, he is walking in the tracks Bony made fifty years ago.[5]

Hillerman's characters, officers Jim Chee and Joe Leaphorn, are Heart and Mind, Yin and Yang: a complementarity that contrasts with and includes the other. Chee is the younger, trained as a medicine man, a singer, hatáli, who maintains a strong connection to Navajo spirituality. Leaphorn is the older, with a degree in anthropology, trained in the ways of Western rationality to be skeptical and to distance himself from tribal traditions.

---

5. de Hoog and Hetherington, eds., *Upfield*, 29.

As they work together to solve the mystery of a crime on the reservation, frequently they must work with the FBI, whose authoritarian, superior, technical approach sees Leaphorn and Chee as uninformed and irrelevant nuisances who just don't understand the proven procedures of investigation.

But in this strange land of sacred traditions, myth and ceremony, the world is in constant flux and decomposition. Dark spirits, witches, skinwalkers seek to overpower the innocent and bring sickness and death. Attaining balance, harmony, hózhó, requires constant attention, courageous hearts and help from medicine men and shamans. This is not a world that dances to government procedures and military protocol. Murder, mayhem, violence, theft, assault are signs that evil forces are pressing the cosmos off-balance into Darkness.

The divergence in the characters of medicine man Jim Chee and the rational, anthropologist Joe Leaphorn becomes less marked as they run into dead-ends in their investigation, and the incompetent FBI gives up.

> It is Hillerman's insistence on "dignity and equality" for his Native characters that makes it possible for them to rise above victimization. Leaphorn and Chee function continually as fully realized Native characters who subtly sabotage the dominant Anglo culture, evincing their superiority to the Anglo power structure and its representatives in both professional expertise and characters.[6]

Leaphorn and Chee must revert to memory of ritual, ceremony and myth for clues to another faint, hidden trail towards the solution of a crime—which, not incidentally, requires a restoration of hózhó. They must return to their communion with the land and read the patterns in the earth and the traces that the creatures leave which give signs and clues for the next step.

In *Dance Hall of the Dead* (1973), Lieutenant Leaphorn investigates the murder of a young Zuni participant in the Shalako winter solstice ceremony at the Zuni Pueblo. Through Leaphorn, Tony Hillerman contrasts and compares the Anglo-secular world, Zuni-Navajo-Roman Catholic spirituality and inductive police procedures. Aggressive, intimidating FBI agents push clumsily through tribal culture and the confessions of two young suspects, assuming that the murder was related to a drug-ring on the Zuni reservation.

---

6. Six, "Slaying the Monsters," 45.

The Dinétah, Arizona-New Mexico — Tony Hillerman

The dynamic differences between the three confessional cultures (syncretic, spiritual and secular) and their different uses and understandings of confession point to the often, but not always, fraught relationships between spirituality, social justice, and secular police work that Hillerman pursues in each of his Navajo detective novels. In *Dance Hall of the Dead*, the Shalako Salamobia dancer figuratively and perhaps literally exacts profound and ultimate justice at the end of the novel, stepping in to assert spiritual and social order when secular law and order failed to do so.[7]

To solve the mystery of violence on the Zuni reservation, Leaphorn must search out Navajo wisdom about nature and landscape, to discern a pattern of clues leading to resolution:

> "When the dung beetle moves," Hosteen Nashibitti had told him, "know that something has moved it. And know that its movement affects the flight of the sparrow, and that the raven deflects the eagle from the sky, and that the eagle's stiff wing bends the will of the Wind People, and know that all of this affects you and me, and the flea on the prairie dog and the leaf on the cottonwood." That had always been the point of the lesson. Interdependency of nature. Every cause has its effect. Every action its reaction. A reason for everything. In all things a pattern, and in this pattern, the beauty of harmony. Thus, one learned to live with evil, by understanding it, but readings its cause. And thus, one learned, gradually and methodically, if one was lucky, to always "go in beauty," To always look for the pattern, and to find it.[8]

This encounter with Hosteen Nahibitti awakened within Leaphorn a primal memory that indeed all things, animate and inanimate, are connected:

> . . . his senses opened to the signs and clues in nature and the landscape that would lead him to resolution. The murders upset the balance and harmony of all things on the Zuni reservation. Nature and landscape would reveal the answer to those who have eyes to see. Ultimately, resolution would not happen in finding and punishing the criminal, but in setting things right.[9]

---

7. Cammack, "Confession and Coercion."
8. Hillerman, *Dance Hall of the Dead*, 77.
9. Reilly, *Tony Hillerman*, 64.

Desert Spirit Places

Hosteen reminded Leaphorn of the Diné myths and parables which explain the nature of things, Native Science if you will. Leaphorn brought this collective memory into his police training. He adapted his root spirituality to the application of rational police science.

In Dance Hall of the Dead, we follow Leaphorn's pursuit of the crime through interviews with people close to the events of the crime. His police training utilizes his rational mind to discover a rational, orderly explanation. And Hillerman gives great weight to the detective's method. At the end of the story, as in most murder mysteries, Detective Leaphorn, reviews all the evidence he found, reflects the narrative of cause and effect revealed in the clues, and solves the crime.

As I reflect on Leaphorn's movement through Diné spiritual roots and rational police investigation procedures, I do not see a dualism in conflict. This is a complementarity, a working-together of opposites which do not contradict each other or cancel each other out, but which include each other.

So, how can I harness mind and heart to read the signs of nature and the signs in my own life? This is a question that is at the center of my journeys into the Sacred Southwest.

Vicarious understanding, perhaps, but still important to me: there are books that can give us clues to finding our way in the wilderness. Here, from one that is particularly useful.

> The roots of a tree indicate the sun's direction; the Big Dipper tells the time; a passing butterfly hints at the weather; a sand dune reveals prevailing wind; the scent of cinnamon suggests altitude; a budding flower points south.[10]

There is a deeper seeing and knowing on this path. Beyond words, there is an engagement with the Book of Nature—with the footsteps of the Holy One beside us.

Joe Leaphorn harnessed mind and heart to make his way through nature's signs, not only to solve a crime, but to restore hózhó and balance, to return to the sacred.

We walk through the landscape in our journey, we reconnect with Nature, establish our kinship, and we enter into communion with the Sacred and see the path ahead to our heart's desires.

---

10. Gooley, *Lost Art of Reading Nature's Signs*, back cover.

The Dinétah, Arizona-New Mexico — Tony Hillerman

> Often I look up into the clouds and daydream about a better world. But my dreams will never bear fruit unless I keep turning my eyes again and again back to the dust of this earth and listen to what God is saying to me on the road of life. For I am connected to the earth and to all who walk the earth with me. Nature is not the background of our lives; it is a living gift that teaches us about the ways and will of the Creator. My friends who are more aware of the way nature teaches have shown me how to slow down and savor the way God's presence is woven into the natural world.[11]

Is that not our common desire as we discern the way ahead: in conflict and desire, in hope and longing, to find harmony, balance, homecoming with the Sacred?

> Instead of theological treatises, Hillerman offers his readers two Navajo tribal policemen who, in answer to the primal need to find wholeness in a re-unification of animus and anima with essential Unity, seek meaningful relationships with the women in their lives, struggle with questions of personal integrity and identity, and emerge as agents of Original Grace. For Leaphorn and Chee, the question is never about professional advancement or money; it is not even about "bringing criminals to justice." For Joe Leaphorn and Jim Chee, the seeking and struggle is about hózhó.[12]

> Hózhó is the path or journey in which we strive for wellness through harmony in relationships, respect and spirituality.[13]

This is the gift of Tony Hillerman: to remind us, Native American and Anglo-American that hózhó is the goal for all of us.

---

11. Nouwen, *Discernment*, 53.
12. Six, "Slaying the Monsters," 209–10.
13. Kahn-John, "Living in Health."

19.

Alabama Hills, California —Desert Night Sky

> One may try to look at the sky, but in fact one looks through it . . . for no matter how deeply one sees into the sky, there is always an infinite depth remaining.
> —Thomas McEvilley[1]

THE GREEN OVERHEAD STREET sign for Whitney Portal Road swings wildly in the November wind, as I wait at the signal on Highway 395 in Lone Pine, California. To my right are local restaurants; Seasons, Merry Go Round, and The Grill—all of which radiate hospitality. They are jammed with skiers heading to and returning from Mammoth Mountain, two hours to the north. My Honda Pilot shudders in the buffeting blasts of wind. With a green light I turn left heading toward Mount Whitney and the Sierra Nevada. Away from the town's lights, dense darkness descends. Suddenly, a tumbleweed the size of a Volkswagen Beetle barrels across the road in front of me.

The road twists and turns, following Lone Pine Creek. Denuded cottonwood and willow trees bend in the whistling wind. More debris flies by. I think to myself that maybe I should not be on this road in such an intense desert windstorm.

I enter the narrows of the Alabama Hills, and the road climbs higher. Gnarled, weirdly shaped boulders cast haunting shadows in my headlights. Having driven this road many times before, I look for familiar clues

---

1. McEvilley, quoted in Anderson, "Embracing the Void."

Alabama Hills, California—Desert Night Sky

to Movie Road. I come upon an open plateau where the wind is blocked out by the hills and rocks, and there I see the sign for Movie Road, turn right and continue north on a half-mile paved section leading to a wide dirt road. I jam on my brakes as a mother doe and two fawn dash across the road.

I might as well park here, and I step out into the dark night. This point is a thousand feet higher than Lone Pine; the town's lights are blocked by the Alabama Hills and I am standing on a plateau on a moonless night. The car and landscape dissolve into the darkness. I am unable to see my feet. Facing east, I see the starry night sky on both sides of me, half a circle. Without reference to the ground or the horizon, I seem to be surrounded by night sky, brilliant, twinkling diamonds of light scattered about me. I feel I am being lifted up into the sky, plunging into the vast Milky Way. The more I focus on the brighter stars, the more the fainter ones become clear. Millions! Infinity. This is a thin place between heaven and earth, between reason and wondrous mystery.

Thomas Merton shares:

> It is a strange awakening to find the sky inside you and beneath you and above you and all around you so that your spirit is one with the sky, and all is positive night.[2]

Others before me have stood in this same place, or in a million other places, all surrounded by night sky, all lifted up into infinity and wonder. This is the birthplace of gods, myths and holy signs. Perhaps I am so staggered, overwhelmed because, I confess, I rarely look at the sky when I am at home. Our night sky is usually occluded by fog and coastal clouds as we are just a couple of miles from the ocean.

One thousand miles east of Lone Pine, at the end of a long, difficult desert road, is Christ in the Desert Benedictine Monastery of Abiquiu, New Mexico. Belden Lane writes:

> That first night at the monastery I went to bed while it was still light, knowing I had to be up early if I was to make it to chapel for Vigils. I lay there, listening to the wind howl as night came on. The desert was dark, cold, and moonless. Unable to sleep, I pulled the sleeping bag around me and waited out the night. When three-thirty finally arrived, I pulled on clothes in the cold morning air and walked outside with a small flashlight. It was pitch black, still

---

2. Merton, *When the Trees Say Nothing*, 87.

completely alone, I nervously felt my way up the canyon toward the chapel.

But as I stopped to lie down on a large rock and look up into the night sky, my uneasiness suddenly dissolved. I was home. The sky was lit with thousands of stars, stars I immediately recognized from my backyard in Saint Louis where I pray every night. Leo the Lion, Bootes the Ox-Driver, Hercules with his arms upraised— they were all there, stretched out across the heavens. A place without comfort or familiarity suddenly revealed itself as home.[3]

Desert night sky. 2013. Photo by ESO/H. Dahle.

For millennia, the night sky has been a celestial canvas on which people have recreated images from myths and sacred stories in their communion with the Sacred. I encountered one night-sky story in an unusual children's book: *Menorah in the Night Sky: A Miracle of Chanukah*, by Jacques J. M. Shore, which I summarize below.

Zev loved the Jewish feast of Chanukah, the gathering of extended family, the holiday foods, gifts and games spread out over eight days. A new candle on the Menorah would be lit over eight days and his home would radiate light and joy. But eleven-year-old Zev and his ten-year-old friend

---

3. Lane, *Solace of Fierce Landscapes*, 221–22.

Alabama Hills, California — Desert Night Sky

David were far from home and family, confined to Auschwitz concentration camp, where they survived by sorting through huge piles of shoes left behind by those who were killed in the gas chambers.

In the growing darkness of winter, Zev's memories of Chanukah returned, and he remembered the lighting of the Menorah each night. When David recalled his own memories of family and Chanukah, it filled him with sadness. Zev began to pray for a miracle.

One night Zev and David looked up into the sky and saw a bright star. They sang a Chanukah song quietly in the night. Each night the boys would go outside of the bleak barracks, light a candle, say a blessing, and each night another star would appear until "a semi-circular shape of eight stars appeared, emerging one after another."

And the story continues:

> The Night after Chanukah was over, the boys took their spot outside the barracks as they had done for the previous eight days. This night, unlike all the others, the sky was filled with millions of stars. Never before had they seen such a star-filled sky. Never before could they have imagined that so many stars could exist.
>
> Zev said, "Those stars are free, so free in the heavens. David believe me—we too will one day be free."
>
> The remnants of light and warmth of Chanukah kept Zev and David alive. Zev explained and promised David that the spirit of Yehuda the Maccabee and the miracle of Chanukah that they share would ensure their survival in the camp.
>
> God, who lit the Menorah in the sky, lit their way out of Auschwitz, a few months later.[4]

Among Native American tribes, the animate and inanimate worlds, the earth and the sky, are one unified, interdependent entity. The stars in the night sky are living spiritual beings. The problem for Anglo-European exploration of these traditions is that in the past these earth-sky stories were suppressed by the dominant Anglo culture. Contemporary probing and inquisitive academic explorations have met native suspicion and resistance toward disclosing the sacred stories. Sharing information about the Sacred dilutes its operative power.

The close relationship between people and the stars in the night sky is illustrated by the Navajo, who see the world and universe holistically,

---

4. Shore, *Menorah in the Night Sky*, 24.

everything is connected in a system of relationships that is in constant flux. While Western science applies rational tools to study the cosmos, Navajo astronomy is at the heart of their spirituality. All things, animate and inanimate, on earth and in the heavens are living entities. Every human action affects this organic universe.

I imagine Carl Sagan, the scientist, standing beside me beholding the desert night sky in the Alabama Hills. I can still hear his voice as he narrated the famous PBS television series *Cosmos: A Personal Journey*. As he guided us into the mysteries of the night sky, he said nothing of a Creator, and nothing of the religious myths about the cosmos. Sagan was a true buffered self, who applied an inquisitive skepticism while rejecting religious dogma.

Sagan was a colleague of my brother, Michael Karelius, when they both worked on the Mariner Project at NASA's Jet Propulsion Laboratory in Pasadena, California.

As we stand together contemplating the Milky Way streaming overhead, I hear Sagan's voice from the television series:

> The Cosmos is all that is or ever was or ever will be. Our feeblest contemplations of the Cosmos stir us—there is a tingling in the spine, a catch in the voice, a faint sensation as if of a distant memory, a falling from a height. We know we are approaching the greatest of mysteries.[5]

For all its clarity and brilliance, the strictly scientific approach to the greatest of mysteries is not the end of the story. In a unique partnership between Western science and Navajo spirituality, NASA and the Navajo Nation have created an astrology curriculum used in schools on the Navajo reservation. The text is called *Navajo Moon: Educational Activities Bringing Together NASA Science and Navajo Cultural Knowledge* (2006). While much of the traditional knowledge of Navajo astronomy has been forgotten, this curriculum is an attempt to knit together dispersed stories and information into a whole. The project was reaffirmed at a meeting between NASA and the Navajo Nation at Window Rock, Arizona in 2005.

Here are two important elements of the Navajo relationship to the creatures of the night sky.

Constellations Provide Guidance and Values: Navajo relationships with the stars can be very personal. Star constellations can be utilized for healing

---

5. Sagan, *Cosmos*.

body, mind and spirit. Many Navajo constellations are depicted in human form, providing principles and values for living.

Stars as Related to Animals and Natural Elements: Many Navajo constellations are directly connected to animals . . . porcupine, gila monster, mountain sheep. Other constellations include natural elements such as flash lightning, the sun, the moon. The stars are also closely related to seasonal vegetation and animal life-processes such as mating and giving birth.

The traditional way to teach Navajo astrology was at home or in the hogan, during the winter months. The families would gather to listen to the elder who knew the most about the stories. But now many details have been forgotten and attempts at reconstructing the stories have led to differing versions. You can review the valuable resource that NASA and the Navajo published as *A Collection of Curricula for the STARLAB Navajo Skies Cylinder*. In this are stories from many elders, collected over several years.

An innovation that replicates the family milieu of the hogan is the Star Lab.

> We have developed a Mylar cylinder for us in the Star Lab, a portable planetarium. Telling oral stories in the darkness of the Star Lab, which resembles the cultural environment of a circular hogan, with music and voice, approximates the traditional Navajo way of passing knowledge.[6]

Another teaching aid is a string game using figures found in the Navajo constellation. The players use the string to recreate the First Man and the First Woman as they attempt to place the stars in the night sky. But then that gets all messed up by the Trickster Coyote.

One story that may well be of particular value to those of non-Native American heritage is the Navajo elder's NASA joke:

> When NASA was preparing for the Apollo Project, it took the astronauts to a Navajo reservation in Arizona for training. One day, a Navajo elder and his son came across the space crew walking among the rocks. The elder, who spoke only Navajo, asked a question. His son translated for the NASA people: "What are these guys in the big suits doing?" One of the astronauts said that they were practicing for a trip to the moon. When his son relayed this comment the Navajo elder got all excited and asked if it would be possible to give to the astronauts a message to deliver to the moon. Recognizing a promotional opportunity when he saw one, a

---

6. Maryboy et al., *Collection of Curricula*, 4.

NASA official accompanying the astronauts said, "Why certainly!" and told an underling to get a tape recorder. The Navajo elder's comments into the microphone were brief.

The NASA official asked the son if he would translate what his father had said. The son listened to the recording and laughed uproariously. But he refused to translate. So the NASA people took the tape to a nearby Navajo village and played it for other members of the tribe. They too laughed long and loudly but also refused to translate the elder's message to the moon.

Finally, an official government translator was summoned. After he finally stopped laughing the translator relayed the message: "Watch out for these assholes—they have come to steal your land."[7]

In *Believing in Place*, Richard Francaviglia contemplates the night sky after midnight in a visit to western Utah. "I'd looked up into the night sky and beheld a Milky Way that looked like crushed glittering glass–or pulverized diamonds–spread from horizon to horizon."

The vast dark sky studded with luminescent lights becomes a canvas for the imagination to "connect the dots" between stars and recreate images and creatures of nature. Francaviglia echoes the imaginative minds of the Navajo, as he writes about the Milky Way and star figures:

> One of nature's most awesome sights, this clustering of millions of stars has deep cultural significance in the Great Basin. The Paiute call it Kus'ipo" (Dusty Trail) or, more to the point, Numu-po (People's Trail), and they believe it to be the path traveled by the souls of the dead as they seek another, more abundant world to the south where there will be good hunting and time for gambling and dancing. The Big Dipper shimmering overhead is Ta'noa'di, a heavenly net into which men chase rabbits. To some Native peoples hereabouts, Orion's belt consists of three stars that are either mountain sheep or mountain sheep husbands, while the brightest star in this constellation (Sirius) is a woman called Tinagidi (The Chaser). Significantly, the heavens themselves are not the product of remote physical forces, but of Wolf (creator of both Heaven and Earth) and his trickster brother Coyote, who caused his family to flee to the sky.[8]

---

7. http://www.rainbowbody.net/Ongwhehonwhe/nasanavajo.htm.
8. Francaviglia, *Believing in Place*, 23.

Alabama Hills, California — Desert Night Sky

It is time for me to return to the warmth of my car and the lights of Lone Pine. I am remembering the thoughts of the seventeenth-century mathematician Blaise Pascal, who, as he also gazed into the dark night sky, exclaimed, "The eternal silence of these infinite spaces frightens me." I leave with a different feeling. I could hear other sounds of nature out there in the darkness that could have triggered anxiety and fear within me. But as the wonder that came from focusing my eyes on the stars, and as each minute went by, the dimensions of the sky and number of stars growing in immensity, I too felt a sense of homecoming, that I was being embraced in love by the Holy Creator.

I lose myself in darkness among mythic star creatures. Until now I have lived a life attentive only to daylight, unaware of the wonders and mystery of this other half of Creation: the pulsing, vibrant, numinous night sky.

20.

Where We Are Now —Second Naiveté

> Beyond the desert of criticism, we wish to be called again.
> —Paul Ricoeur[1]

HOLY SAND THAT HEALS? Stone fetish carvings that are alive? Desert monks who see visions? Wilderness weeds which cure? Entheogens that help you see God? Desert winds that bring sickness?

As we have journeyed together through the desert spirit places of the Southwest, have you changed? Has a deep place within you recognized anything here that has animated your soul?

Can you remember a time in your childhood when you read a book and the stories were so real that your imagination awakened with vivid excitement: all of this truly happened?

Perhaps that book became tattered and worn by your frequent return into the realm of wonder. But as you grew older, the book fell back into a dark recess of the bookshelf. Perhaps, as later you sorted through your childhood memorabilia, the book revealed itself again, and your spirit stirred for a precious moment—but only that, and the book was put back on the shelf or sent to the thrift shop. Or, did you begin to read the story again with new eyes, admiring the dated but so-delicate illustrations, and the round phrases that you had once relished and memorized. With new eyes you read again, and the story becomes alive. Perhaps you are now

---

1. Ricoeur, *Symbolism of Evil*, 349.

reading the book aloud to your child, or grandchild, and the eyes and ears of wonder in that child begin to radiate energy toward you.

This experience could be called "second naiveté," and French philosopher Paul Ricouer helps us to understand its deeper meaning. He breaks the experience into three stages, and I am grateful to Linards Jansons for his insight into them. Rather than on storybooks, Ricouer reflects on sacred texts.

In the Pre-Critical Stage, stories in the Bible such as the Creation, Adam and Eve, and Noah's flood are received as true accounts. The supernatural world is real. This naïve, mythical, perception of the Bible was the norm in Europe until the Enlightenment of the seventeenth century. I would always remind my world religions students that "myth" does not betoken an untrue story. A myth is a story that describes who we are, how we came to be, our relationship to creation and with God.

The Enlightenment shifted the source of knowledge from the Bible to the Book of Nature. As people traveled to new lands, the exposure to other religions challenged rigid Christian orthodoxy. Jewish and Christian scriptures were studied and analyzed in their earlier languages, rather than in the Latin of the Vulgate Bible.

At which point we enter the Critical Stage. There is now a distance between the world described in the Bible and our world. There is distance between the porous, supernatural world and our own buffered world of Reason and the scientific method.

In the late 1960s in seminary, as I prepared to be a parish priest, to teach and apply the spirituality of Jesus and the Bible, I encountered a brittle, dry "desert of criticism" in the classroom. Analysis, suspicion and skepticism seemed to be the dominant positions as we studied the sacred stories of faith. Linards Jansons reflects:

> . . . this is no ordinary desert, but a "desert of criticism," an intellectual desert, part of our Western cultural topography. How did we get there? Should we be there? And who is this "we"? Our Ricoeurian proverb suggests that whoever "we" are, we are ready to move on. We wish to be "called," but by whom? And why "again"? When was the first time? And why beyond the "desert"? Where are we now being called? Back from whence we came, or on to a new place?[2]

2. Jansons, "What Is the Second Naiveté?"

For many of us, the "what next?" has faded away. We are distracted by enticing diversions. For some the Sacred has no meaning because the pre-critical stories were never told in the first place, or skepticism and reason killed the faith. But I am convinced of the power of a Holy Longing, the deep desire within every human for direct, personal connection to the Sacred, and surely the stories, the myths, now informed by who we have become, can lead us there.

Ricouer's Post-Critical Moment suggests that we work with and carry the gifts of Reason and textual criticism; we explore the anthropology behind the text, story and sacred tradition; we consider explanations that speak to the world we live in now; and we continue the journey, which is now an inner, intuitive, mystical path. All critical insights are welcome. We are not going back to the pre-critical medieval Europe. We are not stuck in the skeptical desert. We press on. I believe that the "call beyond" of Ricoeur is an inner voice that seeks to awaken inner eyes to perceive the sacred.

My friend and teacher Walter Brueggemann shares:

> I was educated in historical criticism, as everyone was, to keep the text in the past and to presume that it had one recoverable meaning intended by the author. It became clear to me that I had to find a way, while taking historical criticism seriously, to move beyond it. By accident, I started reading about the theory of the imagination with reference to Paul Ricoeur. That led me to see that what we always do with the biblical text, if we want it to be pertinent or compelling or contemporary, is commit mostly unrecognized acts of imagination by which we stretch and pull and extend the implications of the text beyond its words.[3]

In the late 1960s, amid a great cultural upheaval in the United States, I entered seminary in Berkeley, California. The Episcopal Church did not know what to do with young adult males who had experienced any kind of spiritual awakening, so the Church sent us to seminary. Many of us came from that Pre-Critical Phase, with a naïve understanding of the Bible and sacraments. In seminary we faced the Critical Stage head-on. The old orthodoxy that the first five books of the Bible were written by Moses (among many other ideas) was replaced by Form Criticism, and the theory that various authors writing at various times wrote the Pentateuch. As we studied the Gospels, we encountered scholars questioning the kerygma (core-proclamations) that really did come from Jesus and the overlay of tradition coming from the early Church.

---

3. Winters, "Conversation with Walter Brueggemann."

We were taught to be rigorous academics, which fostered a dispassionate, distant skepticism in us.

In 1970, I began parish ministry in Laguna Beach, California, amid hippy drug culture and my first encounters with homeless people and poor immigrants. Ministry pulled me out of the sanctuary and into the community to respond to the needs of people who might not show up at church—as St. Francis of Assisi taught, "Preach the Gospel at all times; when necessary use words."

My first twenty years of preaching sermons was more of an academic exercise than anything else: exegesis, hermeneutical research on the cultural context of the scripture at the time it was written, and how to apply those teachings to our own lives, with witty anecdotes thrown in. That all changed in 1990 when I began spiritual direction with Sister Jeanne Fallon of the Sisters of St. Joseph of Orange. At a very troubled, depressing time of life, in the first few years after Erik's catastrophic illness, I was searching, and an inner voice was calling me forward.

Sister Jeanne encouraged me to begin the year-long program of the Spiritual Exercises, created five hundred years ago by St. Ignatius of Loyola, a Spanish mystic. So, it began. The curriculum involved meditating every day on a passage from the Bible. After an initial period of deep self-reflection on my humanity and relationship to the Creator, I progressed into the life, death and resurrection of Jesus. After reading the assigned scripture, I would sit in silence for thirty minutes every day, inviting Jesus to be with me to open my imagination and to draw me into the scripture. This was not a calming experience! Rather, inner conflicts, anger and grief bubbled to the surface like flotsam and jetsam after a shipwreck. After each meditation I wrote down in a journal what I heard God saying to me. I would meet with Sister Jeanne every week to reflect on what this encounter with Scripture and Jesus meant to me.

This year of meditation changed my life. The old skeptical distance faded. I had direct experience of the presence of God in Jesus. I listened to the words of Jesus as if they were spoken for me to hear today, for the first time. We are "called again" to the place of wonder that we once knew many years ago. Ron Rolheiser shares:

> We do this by making a deliberate and conscious effort at assuming the posture of a child before reality. We must work at regaining

the primal spirit, a sense of wonder, the sense that reality is rich and full of mystery, that we do not yet understand and that we must read chastely, carefully, and discriminately, respecting reality's contours and taboos. Concomitant with this effort comes the deliberate and conscious attempt at purging ourselves of all traces of cynicism, contempt, and all attitudes which identify mystery with ignorance, taboo with superstition, and romance and ideals with naiveté.[4]

In our visits to these desert spirit places, asking for the Holy Presence to be with us, in silence and solitude, our primal senses will open in remembrance of our natural communion with all things.

The English writer of the 1930s G. K. Chesterton created this poem:

A Second Childhood
When all my days are ending
And I have no song to sing,
I think I shall not be too old
To stare at everything;
As I stared once at a nursery door
Or a tall tree and a swing...[5]

I have my own guide into second naiveté in our disabled son Erik. I am walking with Erik after dinner. It is a familiar routine: a one-mile saunter around the Big Block. But this particular night seems to be magical, a night when anything could happen—we are in a thin place between Earth and Heaven. The full golden October moon rises over the hillside to our right. I hold Erik's hand because his gait is unsteady. Although his brain is heavily scarred by disease, he has remarkably strong hearing. Every slight sound stimulates his response: he chuckles at a breaking branch; he gives a sour frown at a barking dog. He hears everything. He says little as we walk but his senses are on high alert. There is mystery and wonder out there in the darkness. As we walk around the Big Block our orientation to the moon changes. Several times we stop and look up at the starry night. "Where is the moon now, Erik?"

"Over there." He points with his finger.

We walk on into the night-blooming jasmine-scented night.

"Where is the moon now, Erik?"

"Over there."

"Erik, did you move the moon again?"

He raises his index finger upward to the moon and moves it.

---

4. Rolheiser, "Saying 'Yes' to Santa Claus."
5. Chesterton, *Ballad of St. Barbara*, 40.

"I like it!"

May your own journey through these desert spirit places of the Southwest awaken memories of innocence and the feeling that at long last you have come home!

Erik Karelius with Harry Nez, Mystery Valley, Utah. 2015. Photo by author.

Bibliography

Abbey, Edward. *The Best of Edward Abbey.* San Francisco: Sierra Club Books, 1984.
Aggarwal-Schifellite, Manisha. "I Want to Believe." *The Oyster Review,* October 2015. http://review.oysterbooks.com/p/q026fhAMSULNELZaWj6yQn/i-want-to-believe
Agosin, Thomas. "Mysticism and Psychosis." *Seeds of Unfolding* 6, no. 4 (Fall 1989). http://http://www.seedsofunfolding.org/issues/11_08/feature_english.htm.
Allen, Paul. "Old Twists on Dust Devils." *Tucson Citizen,* July 3, 1996. http://tucsoncitizen.com/morgue2/1996/07/03/186880-old-twists-on-dust-devils/.
Anderson, Ross. "Embracing the Void." *Aeon*, October 15, 2013. https://aeon.co/essays/the-one-place-where-it-s-possible-to-truly-see-the-night-sky.
Austin, Mary. *Land of Little Rain.* New York: Houghton, Mifflin, 1903.
Bahti, Mark. *Spirit in Stone: A Handbook of Southwest Indian Animal Carvings and Beliefs.* Tucson, AZ: Rio Nuevo, 2016.
Barnett, Ray, and Linda Martin. *Spruce Tree House.* Mesa Verde National Park, CO: Mesa Verde Museum Association, 2014.
Begay, Rudy. "Avert Your Eyes: Eclipse Viewing Taboo in Navajo and Other Cultures." *Indian Country Today,* May 20, 2012. https://newsmaven.io/indiancountrytoday/archive/avert-your-eyes-eclipse-viewing-taboo-in-navajo-and-other-cultures-aSQi5i4mPEqVo-K7IVuhbw/.
Berman, Marshall. *All That Is Solid Melts into the Air: The Experience of Modernity.* New York: Penguin, 1988.
Beyer, Stephan V. *Singing to the Plants: A Guide to Mestizo Shamanism in the Upper Amazon.* Albuquerque: University of New Mexico Press, 2010.
Blake, John, and Charles Brand, executive producers. *The Monastery.* Documentary series about Christ in the Desert Monastery. BBC, 2005.
Bowers, Janice Emily. *Fish Springs and Black Rock: Forgotten Towns of Owens Valley.* N.p.: Three Gardens, 2014.
Brown, Patricia Leigh. "A Disease without a Cure Spreads in the West." *New York Times*, July 4, 2013. http://www.nytimes.com/2013/07/05/health/a-disease-without-a-cure-spreads-quietly-in-the-west.html.
Brueggemann, Walter. "Where Is the Scribe?" *Anglican Theological Review* 93, no. 3, 385–403. http://www.anglicantheologicalreview.org/static/pdf/articles/brueggemann.pdf
Buber, Martin. *I and Thou.* Translated by Ronald Gregor Smith. New York: Scribner, 1958.
Burton-Christie, Douglas. *The Word in the Desert: Scripture and the Quest for Holiness in Early Christian Monasticism.* Oxford: Oxford University Press, 1993.

Bibliography

Cammack, Emily. "Confession and Coercion in Tony Hillerman's DANCE HALL OF THE DEAD." Facebook post, June 3, 2014. https://www.facebook.com/TonyHillermanPortal/posts/496309137167957.

Chesterton, Gilbert Keith, *The Ballad of St. Barbara and Other Verses.* London: Cecil Palmer, 1922.

Chitty, Dewas. *The Desert a City: An Introduction to the Study of Egyptian and Palestinian Monasticism Under the Christian Empire.* Yonkers, NY: St. Vladimir's Seminary Press, 1966.

Chryssavgis, John. *In the Heart of the Desert: The Spirituality of the Desert Fathers and Mothers.* Bloomington, IN: World Wisdom, 2008.

Clark, H. Jackson. *The Owl in the Canyon: And Other Stories from Indian Country.* Salt Lake City: University of Utah Press, 1993.

Coles, Robert. *The Spiritual Life of Children.* Boston: Houghton Mifflin, 1990.

Comerford, Michael Sean. "Incredible Story of Navajo Mike, Child of the Dust Devil Air." *The Blog, HuffPost*, May 14, 2013. https://www.huffpost.com/entry/incredible-story-of-navaj_b_3187055.

Cushing, Frank. *Zuni Fetishes.* Facsimile of 1883 ed. Las Vegas: K.C. Publications, 1990

Daggy, Tobert. *Thomas Merton: The Desert Call.* Santa Fe, NM: Merton Center, 1993.

de Hoog, Kees, and Carol Hetherington, editors. *Upfield: The Man Who Started It. Investigating Arthur Upfield: A Centenary Collection of Critical Essays.* Cambridge: Cambridge Scholars, 2011.

Dillard, Annie. *Pilgrim at Tinker Creek.* New York: Harper and Row, 1974.

"Don Mose - Navajo Spirit tour guide - Mystery Valley." YouTube video, March 12, 2017. https://www.youtube.com/watch?v=6rcqwN7-scI.

Eliot, T. S. *East Coker, Four Quartets.* Boston: Mariner, 1968.

———. *The Wasteland.* New York: Modern Library Classics, 2002.

Flores, Dan. *Horizontal Yellow: Nature and History in the Near Southwest.* Albuquerque: University of New Mexico Press, 1999.

Francaviglia, Richard V. *Believing in Place: A Spiritual Geography of the Great Basin.* Reno: University of Nevada Press, 2003.

Finch, Robert, editor. *The Norton Book of Nature Writing.* New York: Norton, 2002.

Foster, Joseph. *D. H. Lawrence in Taos.* Albuquerque: University of New Mexico Press, 1972.

Gardner, Jason, editor. *The Sacred Earth: Writers on Nature and Spirit.* Novato, CA: New World Library, 1998.

Gooley, Tristan. *The Lost Art of Reading Nature's Signs.* New York: The Experiment, 2014.

Grady, Wayne, editor. *Desert: A Literary Companion.* Vancouver: Greystone, 2008.

Greenberg, Martin, editor. *The Tony Hillerman Companion: A Comprehensive Guide to His Life and Work.* New York: HarperCollins, 1994.

Griffen-Pierce, Trudy. *Earth Is My Mother, Sky Is My Father: Space, Time and Astronomy in Navajo Sand Paintings.* Albuquerque: University of New Mexico Press, 1992.

Griffith, James S. *Beliefs and Holy Places: A Spiritual Geography of the Pimería Alta.* Tucson: University of Arizona Press, 1992.

Grof, Stanislav. *Psychology of the Future.* Albany, NY: SUNY Press, 2000.

Gruber, Mark. *Journey Back to Eden: My Life and Times Among the Desert Fathers.* Maryknoll, NY: Orbis, 2002.

Guignard, Lilace Mellin. *A Field Guide to the Norton Book of Nature Writing.* New York: Norton, 2002.

Bibliography

H., Alan. "Monastery of Christ in the Desert 2016." YouTube video, August 21, 2016. https://www.youtube.com/watch?v=ATHGucXThm4.

Harvey, Thomas J. *Rainbow Bridge to Monument Valley: Making the Modern Old West.* Norman: University of Oklahoma Press, 2003.

Hillerman, Anne. *Cave of Bones: A Leaphorn, Chee, and Manuelito Novel.* New York: Harper, 2018.

———. *Tony Hillerman's Landscape: On the Road with Chee and Leaphorn.* Photography by Don Strel. New York: HarperCollins, 2009.

Hillerman, Tony. *Dance Hall of the Dead.* New York: HarperCollins, 2009.

———. *Indian Country: America's Sacred Land.* Photography by Bela Kalman. Weston, MA: Yearout Editions, 1987.

———. "Our Own Holy Land." *Louis L'Amour Western Magazine*, premiere issue (1993) 83–89.

Hirst, Stephen. *Life in a Narrow Place.* New York: David McKay, 1976.

Huxley, Aldous. *A Brave New World.* New York: Everyman's Library, 2013.

———. "The Desert of Perception." In *Complete Essays*, vol. 5, *1939–1956*, edited by Robert S. Baker and James Sexton. Chicago: Ivan R. Dee, 2002.

———. *The Doors of Perception.* New York: Harper and Row, 1954.

———. "The Double Crisis." *UNESCO Courier,* April 1949.

Iliff, Flora Gregg. *People of the Blue Water: A Record of Life Among the Walapai and Havasupai Indians.* Tucson: University of Arizona Press, 1985.

James, William. *Varieties of Religious Experience.* New York: Modern Library, 1999.

Jansons, Linards. Online: "What Is the Second Naiveté?: Engaging with Paul Ricoeur, Post-Critical Theology, and Progressive Christianity." Presentation given to the teaching faculty of Australian Lutheran College, October 30, 2014. http://www.academia.edu/14690650/What_is_the_Second_Naivet%C3%A9_Engaging_with_Paul_Ricoeur_Post-Critical_Theology_and_Progressive_Christianity.

Jasper, David. *The Sacred Desert: Religion, Literature, Art, and Culture.* Oxford: Blackwell, 2004.

Johnston, P. J. "Psychiatric Drugs and Healing." *America,* April 22, 2014.

Johnston, William. *Silent Music: The Science of Meditation.* New York: Harper and Row, 1974.

Jung, C. G. *Memories, Dreams, Reflections.* Recorded and edited by Aniela Jaffé, translated from the German by Richard and Clara Winston. New York: Vintage, 1963.

Kahn-John, Michelle. "Living in Health, Harmony and Beauty." *Global Advances in Health and Medicine* 4, no. 3 (May 2015) 24–30. https://www.ncbi.nlm.nih.gov/pmc/articles/PMC4424938/.

Karelius, Brad. *Encounters with the World Religions: The Numinous on Highway 395.* Eugene, OR: Wipf & Stock, 2015.

———. *The Spirit in the Desert: Pilgrimages to Sacred Sites in the Owens Valley.* Charleston, SC: Booksurge, 2009.

Kavanagh, James, et al. *A Pocket Naturalist Guide to Medicinal Plants.* Duniden, FL: Waterford, 2002.

Keneally, Thomas. *The Place Where Souls Are Born: A Journey into the American Southwest.* New York: Simon and Schuster, 1992.

Kirk, Ruth F. *Zuni Fetishism.* Albuquerque, NM: Avanyu, 1988.

Kluckhohn, Clyde, and Dorothea Leighton. *The Navajo.* Cambridge, MA: Harvard University Press, 1946.

Bibliography

Kluckhohn, Clyde. *Navajo Witchcraft*. Boston: Beacon, 1967.

Krafel, Paul. *Seeing Nature: Deliberate Encounters with the Visible World*. White River Junction, VT: Chelsea Green, 1999.

Krutch, Joseph Wood. *The Desert Year*. Tucson: University of Arizona Press, 1985.

Lane, Belden. *Landscape of the Sacred: Geography and Narrative in American Spirituality*. Baltimore: Johns Hopkins University Press, 2002.

———. *The Solace of Fierce Landscapes: Exploring Desert and Mountain Spirituality*. Oxford: Oxford University Press, 1998.

Lanner, Ronald. *The Pinon Pine: A Natural and Cultural History*. Reno: University of Nevada Press, 1981.

Lewis, C. S. *The Four Loves*. New York: HarperOne, 2017.

Luhan, Mabel Dodge. *Edge of Taos Desert: An Escape to Reality*. Albuquerque: University of New Mexico Press, 1987.

Lummis, Charles. *The Land of Poco Tiempo*. Albuquerque: University of New Mexico Press, 1969.

Martin, James. "Holy Dirt: A Pilgrimage to Chimayo, the Lourdes of America." *America Magazine*, February 25, 2008. https://www.americamagazine.org/issue/646/article/holy-dirt.

Maryboy, Nancy C. *Navajo Skies: A guide to Navajo Astronomy*. Bluff, UT: Indigenous Education Institute, 2004.

Maryboy, Nancy C., and David Begay. *Sharing the Skies: Navajo Astronomy*. Tucson, AZ: Rio Nuevo, 1991.

Maryboy, Nancy C., et al. *A Collection of Curricula for the STARLAB Navajo Skies Cylinder*. Buffalo, NY: Science First/STARLAB, 2008.

Mashberg, Tom. "Despite Legal Challenges, Sale of Hopi Religious Artifacts Continues in France." *New York Times*, June 30, 2014. https://www.nytimes.com/2014/06/30/arts/design/sale-of-hopi-religious-items-continues-despite-us-embassys-efforts.html.

Matthiessen, Peter. *Indian Country*. New York: Viking, 1984.

May, Gerald G. *The Wisdom of Wilderness: Experiencing the Healing Power of Nature*. New York: HarperCollins, 2006.

Mayes, Vernon, and Barbara Bayless Lacy. *Nanise': A Navajo Herbal: One Hundred Plants from the Navajo Reservation*. Chandler, AZ: Five Star, 2012.

McManis, Kent. *Zuni Fetishes and Carvings*. Tucson, AZ: Rio Nuevo, 2004.

McPherson, Robert S. *Sacred Land Sacred View: Navajo Perceptions of the Four Corners*. Salt Lake City: Brigham Young University Press, Charles Redd Center for Western Studies, 1995.

Merton, Thomas. *Bread in the Wilderness*. New York: New Directions, 1997.

———. *The Monastery of Christ in the Desert*. Unpublished essay.

———. *The School of Charity: Letters*. New York: MacMillan, 1990.

———. *Thoughts in Solitude*. New York: Dell, 1961.

———. *When the Trees Say Nothing: Writings on Nature*. Notre Dame, IN: Sorin, 2008.

———. *The Wisdom of the Desert*. New York: New Directions, 1960.

———. *Woods, Shore, Desert*. Santa Fe: Museum of New Mexico Press, 1982.

Momaday, N. Scott. *The Man Made of Words: Essays, Stories, Passages*. New York: St. Martin's, 1997.

Moon, William Least Heat. *Blue Highways: A Journey into America*. Boston: Little, Brown, 1982.

Bibliography

Muslim, Imam Abul-Husain. *Sahih Muslim*. Translated by Abdul Hamid Siddiqui. Saudi Arabia: Dar-Us-Salam, 2007. https://muflihun.com/muslim/23/5084.

Nabokov, Peter. *Where the Lightning Strikes: The Lives of American Indian Sacred Places*. New York: Penguin, 2006.

National Aeronautics and Space Administration, and Navajo Nation. *Navajo Moon: Educational Activities Bringing Together NASA Science and Navajo Cultural Knowledge*. NASA, 2006.

Napier, Jonathan. "Interfaith Dialogue Theory and Native/Non-Native Relations." *Illumine* 10, no. 1 (2011) 77–90. https://journals.uvic.ca/index.php/Illumine/article/download/10738/2912.

Nelson, Steffie. "Aldous Huxley's Brave New World." *Los Angeles Review of Books*, November 22, 2013.

Niederman, Sharon. *Signs and Shrines: Spiritual Journeys Across New Mexico*. Woodstock NY: Countryman, 2012.

Norman, Russell, translator. *The Lives of the Desert Fathers: The Historia Monachorum in Aegypto*. Oxford: Mowbray, 1980.

Nouwen, Henri. *Discernment: Reading the Signs of Daily Life*. New York: HarperOne, 2013.

O'Donnell, Jim. "The Boundaries of the Sacred: A Visited to Zuni Pueblo Part 1." *VRAI Magazine*, April 18, 2015. https://www.vraimagazine.com/visit-zuni-pueblo/.

O'Reilly, Sean, James O'Reilly, and Tim O'Reilly, editors. *The Road Within: True Stories of Transformation and the Soul*. Palo Alto, CA: Travelers' Tales, 2002.

Otto, Rudolph. *The Idea of the Holy*. Translated by John Harvey. London: Oxford University Press, 1923.

Pacheco, Ana. *A History of Spirituality in Santa Fe: The City of Holy Faith*. Charleston, SC: History Press, 2016.

Paulsell, William O. *Rules for Prayer*. New York: Paulist, 1993.

Paya, Lemuel. *Life in a Narrow Place*. Reno: University of Nevada Press, 1981.

Pirlo, Paolo O. *My First Book of Saints*. Sons of Mary Immaculate, Parañaque City, Philippines: Quality Catholic, 2014.

Plotkin, Bill. *Nature and the Human Soul: Cultivating Wholeness and Community in a Fragmented World*. Novato, CA: New World Library, 2008.

Porter, Joy, editor. *The Cambridge Companion to Native American Literature*. Cambridge: Cambridge University Press, 2005.

Pulido, Alberto. *The Sacred World of the Penitentes*. Washington, DC: Smithsonian Institute, 2000.

Reilly, John M. *Tony Hillerman: A Critical Companion*. Westport, CT: Greenwood, 1996.

Ricoeur, Paul. *The Symbolism of Evil*. Translated by Emerson Buchanan. Boston: Beacon, 1969.

Rolheiser, Ronald. "Contemplative Sound Bytes." Untitled blog, June 23, 2013. http://ronrolheiser.com/contemplative-sound-bytes/#.W-NpORNKiRu.

———. "The Desert, a Place of Preparation." Untitled blog, March 12, 2000. http://ronrolheiser.com/the-desert-a-place-of-preparation/#.W8-K2WhKjE4.

———. "Eucharist as New Manna." Untitled blog, March 3, 2011. http://ronrolheiser.com/eucharist-as-new-manna/#.W8-LT2hKjE4.

———. *The Holy Longing: The Search for a Christian Spirituality*. New York: Doubleday, 1999.

———. "Honesty as Sobriety." Untitled blog, August 31, 2008. http://ronrolheiser.com/honesty-as-sobriety/#.W8-M02hKjE4.

Bibliography

———. "In Exile." Untitled blog, November 9, 1994. http://ronrolheiser.com/in-exile/#.W8-NCGhKjE4.

———. "Longing Is Our Spiritual Lot." Untitled blog, May 2, 1987. http://ronrolheiser.com/longing-is-our-spiritual-lot/#.W8-NeGhKjE4.

———. "Saying 'Yes' to Santa Claus." Untitled blog, May 3, 1984. http://ronrolheiser.com/saying-yes-to-santa-claus/#.W8-N0mhKjE4.

———. "To Live in the Light." Untitled blog, April 22, 2012. http://ronrolheiser.com/to-live-in-the-light/#.W8-NPGhKjE4.

Ruck, Carl, et al. "Entheogens." *Journal of Psychedelic Drugs* 11, nos. 1–2 (1979) 145–46.

Sagan, Carl. *Cosmos*. New York: Random House, 1980.

Savage, Emmy. "Drug Trials: A Letter in Response to Oliver Sacks's Article (August 27, 2012)." *New Yorker*, October 1, 2012. https://www.newyorker.com/magazine/2012/10/01/drug-trials.

Sheldrake, Phillip. *Spaces for the Sacred: Place, Memory, and Identity*. Baltimore: Johns Hopkins University Press, 2001.

Shepard, Paul. *Man in the Landscape: A Historic View of the Esthetics of Nature*. Athens: University of Georgia Press, 2002.

Shore, Jacques J. *Menorah in the Night Sky: A Miracle of Chanukah*. Jerusalem: Gefen, 2003.

Shoumatoff, Alex. *Legends of the American Desert: Sojourns in the Greater Southwest*. New York: Knopf, 1997.

Silko, Leslie Marmon. *Ceremony*. New York: Penguin, 2006.

Six, Beverly G. "Slaying the Monsters: Native American Spirituality in the Works of Tony Hillerman." PhD dissertation, Texas Tech University, May 1998.

Smith, Jeffrey S. "Los Hermanos Penitentes: An Illustrative Essay." *North American Geographer* 2, no. 1 (2000) 70–84.

Smithson, Carma Lee, and Robert Euler. *Havasupai Legends: Religion and Mythology of the Havasupai Indians of the Grand Canyon*. Salt Lake City: University of Utah Press, 1994.

Snyder, Gary. *The Practice of the Wild*. Berkeley, CA: Counterpoint, 1990.

Stahlman, Sandra. "The Relationship between Schizophrenia and Mysticism: A Bibliographic Essay." 1992. https://www.meta-religion.com/Psychiatry/Mysticism/Schizophrenia_Mysticism.htm.

Stevenson, Matilda Croxe. *Ethnobotany of the Zuni Indians*. Washington, DC: Government Printing Office, Bureau of American Ethnology, 1915.

Stilgoe, John R. *Outside Lies Magic: Regaining History and Awareness in Everyday Places*. New York: Walker, 1995.

———. *What Is Landscape?* Cambridge, MA: MIT Press, 2015.

Strehlow, Wighard. *Hildegard of Bingen's Medicine*. Santa Fe, NM: Bear, 1987.

Swanson, John L. *Communing with Nature: A Guidebook for Enhancing Your Relationship with the Living Earth*. Bloomington, IN: 1st Book Library, 2001.

Taylor, Carl N. "Agony in Mexico." *Today Magazine*, 1936.

Taylor, Charles. "Buffered and Porous Selves." *The Immanent Frame*, September 2, 2008. https://tif.ssrc.org/2008/09/02/buffered-and-porous-selves/.

———. *A Secular Age*. Cambridge, MA: Belknap Press at Harvard University, 2007.

Underhill, Evelyn. *Mysticism*. London: Forgotten Books, 2017.

———. *Mystics of the Church*. New York: Aeterna, 2015.

Traub, George, editor. *An Ignatian Spirituality Reader*. Chicago: Loyola, 2008.

Bibliography

Van Dyke, John C. *The Desert: Further Studies in Natural Appearances*. Baltimore: Johns Hopkins University Press, 1999.

Walker, Melissa. *Living on Wilderness Time: 200 Days Alone in America's Wild Places*. Charlottesville, NC: University of Virginia Press, 2002.

Wallace, David Rains. *Chuckwalla Land: The Riddle of California's Desert*. Berkeley: University of California Press, 2011.

Wallace, Mark I. *The Second Naivete: Barth, Ricoeur and the New Yale Theology*. Macon, GA: Mercer University Press, 1990.

Walters, Kerry. *Soul and Wilderness: A Desert Spirituality*. Mahwah, NJ: Paulist, 2001.

Ward, Sister Benedicta. *The Desert Christian: The Sayings of the Desert Fathers*. New York: Penguin, 2003.

Watson, Editha L. *Navajo Sacred Places*. Navajoland Publications 5. Window Rock, AZ: Navajoland, November 1964.

Weber, Steven A., and P. David Seaman, editors. *Havasupai Habitat: A. F. Whiting's Ethnology of a Traditional Indian Culture*. Tucson: University of Arizona Press, 1985.

Weigle, Martha. *Brothers of Light, Brothers of Blood: The Penitentes of the Southwest*. Santa Fe, NM: Ancient City, 1988.

———. editor. *The Penitentes of the Southwest*. Santa Fe, NM: Ancient City, 1970.

Weiner, Michael A. *Earth Medicine—Earth Food: Plant Remedies, Drugs, and Natural Foods of the North American Indians*. New York: Ballantine, 1990.

Welland, Michael. *The Desert: Lands of Lost Border*. London: Reaktion, 2015.

Wild, Peter, editor. *The Desert Reader*. Salt Lake City: University of Utah Press, 1991.

Wild, Peter, editor. *The New Desert Reader: Descriptions of America's Arid Regions*. Salt Lake City: University of Utah Press, 2006.

Wilkes, Paul, and Audrey Glynn, directors. *Merton: A Film Biography*. Firstrun Features, 1984.

Williams, Florence. *The Nature Fix*. New York: Norton, 2017.

Winters, Bradford. "A Conversation with Walter Brueggemann." *Image* 55. https://imagejournal.org/article/conversation-walter-brueggemann/.

Witt, Greg. *Exploring Havasupai: A Guide to the Heart of the Grand Canyon*. Birmingham, AL: Menasha Ridge, 2017.

Woodbury, Richard B. *Sixty Years of Southwestern Archaeology: A History of the Pecos Conference*. Albuquerque: University of New Mexico Press, 1993.

Index

Abiquiu, New Mexico, 46, 48–51, 135–36
addictions, 55–56
Aggarwal-Schifellite, Manisha, 127
"Agony in Mexico" (Taylor), 98
Agosin, Tomas, 69–71
Alcoholics Anonymous (AA), 55
Alpert, Richard (Ram Dass), 123
American Occidentalism, 77
Anasazi ruin, 76, 78, 103
Anderson, Gillian, 126–27
animals, in sacred rituals, 32–39
Anthony of Egypt (saint), 45
Anthony of the Desert, 96
Arco, Alonso de, 69
artistic communities, 34–35, 62
ascetical practices, 94–97
Augustine (saint), 80
Austin, Mary, 17

Bagaviova (native god), 12
Begay, Rudy, 103
Believing in Place (Francaviglia), 140
Belizean community, 5, 44
Benedict of Nursia (saint), 43–44
Benedict's Rule, 48
Berman, Marshall, 77
Bernardo Abeyta, Don, 22
Berra, Yogi, 87
Bible stories, 143, 144
Big Jim (chief), 12
Bonhoeffer, Dietrich, 43
Bowers, Janice Emily, 84
bramble leaves, as medicine, 107
Brave New World (Huxley), 95, 120

bread, spirituality of, 15–16
Breeden, Philip, 59
Bruggemann, Walter, 53, 144
Bryne (archbishop), 97
Buber, Martin, 29, 89, 90–91
"buffered self," 6–7, 37, 39, 106, 138

Campbell, Joseph, 65
Carter, Chris, 127
Carter, Howard, 21
Casler, Alonzo, 83–84
Castaneda, Carlos, 122–23
Catholic Worker ministry, 5, 66
Chesterton, G. K., 89, 146
Christ in the Desert at Abiquiu, New Mexico., 46, 48–51, 135–36
Clifford, Arnold, 103
Clovis people, 3
coccidioidomycosis (valley fever), 20–21
Coles, Robert, 63–64
A Collection of Curricula for the STARLAB Navajo Skies Cylinder, 138–39
Comerford, Michael Sean, 20
Constantine (Roman emperor), 43
constellations, of the Navajo Nation, 138–39, 140
contemplative awareness, 92
corn seeds, 60
Coronado y Lujan, Francisco Vazquez de, 32
Cosmos: A Personal Journey (television series), 138
A Course in Miracles (Schucman), 68

Index

Critical Stage, 143
Crowley, Aleister, 121
Curtis, Edward S., 31, 60, 63
Cushing, Frank Hamilton, 33

Daggy, Robert, 47
Dance Hall of the Dead (Hillerman), 130–32
Davis, Cov and John, 113–15
Deleeuw, Chad, 30
Descartes, René, 6, 37
Desert Fathers and Mothers, 45–47
desert monks, 46, 48–51, 94–100, 135–36
desert night sky, 134–141
"desert of criticism," 143
Dillard Annie, 88, 91
Diné culture, 74–76, 103, 106, 109
Diné language, 80
Dinétah (scared land), 128
dis-ease, 6, 28, 80, 85, 109
drug-induced experiences, 121–24
Duchovny, David, 126
dust devils, 17–21

earth medicine, 105–12
eclipse of the moon or sun, 101–4
Edge of Taos Desert (Luhan), 115–16
El Sanctuario de Chimayo, 22–30, 99–100
Encounter approach, 90
English Book of Common Prayer, 28
Enlightenment era, 143
entheogens, 121–24
Eucharist, 15–16, 30
Evil Way Medicine (Navajo spiritual medication), 107–8
Examen of Conscience, 56–57
Experience approach, 90

Fadiman, Anne, 110
Fallon, Jeanne, 54–56, 145
Ferlinghetti, Lawrence, 49
Ferranti, Philip, 7
fetishes, Zuni Pueblo, 33–35, 39
Filter Theory of Naranjo, 124
Ford, John, 76
Form Criticism, 144

Fort Apache (film), 76
Francaviglia, Richard, 19, 140
Francis of Assisi (saint), 145
Frank, Anne, 85

Germany, Christian spirituality in, 40–43
gold mines, California, 83–84, 98
Good Friday, 99
gratitude, 29–30
Greely, Andrew, 68
Griffen-Pierce, Trudy, 101

Hands Together—A Center for Children, 4–5
Harriman, Job, 120
Harvey, Thomas J., 77
Havasupai Falls, 10
Havasupai people
    Episcopal mission, 11–12
    pinyon seeds, 13–15
    valley fever, 20–21
    water project, 9–11
healing mass, at St. Mary's, Laguna Beach, 28
healing shrine. *See* El Sanctuario de Chimayo
Heat-Moon, William Least, 19
Hebrew people, 14–15
Henkel, Alice, 111
herbal medicine, 106–10
hermits, 47
Hillerman, Tony, 60, 127–133
historical criticism, 144
Holy Longing, 6–7, 144
Holy Sand, 23–27, 30
Holy Spirit, 15
Holy Thursday, 15
Holy Week (1995), 27–28
honesty and transparency, 56
Hopi community, 59–64, 111, 113
House of Prayer Retreat Center, Orange, California, 52–58
hózhó, 130, 132–33
Huxley, Aldous, 95, 119, 120–21

I and Thou (Ich und Dich) (Buber), 90

Index

"I Want to Believe" (Aggarwal-Schifellite), 127
The Idea of the Holy (Otto), 70
Ignatius of Loyola (saint), 7, 38, 54, 145
illumination, seeing vs., 88
"immanent frame," 36
Indian Country (journal), 103
Indian Swap Meet, 106-7
ineffable, defined, 67

J. W. Powell Expedition, 33
James, William, 67, 68, 91-92
Jansons, Linards, 143
Johnston, P. J., 110
Johnston, William, 68, 124

kachina dances, 63
Kai (Willow Tree) Totsonnie, 110-12
Karelius, Brad
    background, 4-5, 28
    debt and adiction, 55
    eye surgery, 87-88
    parish ministry, 145
    prostate cancer, 8, 29-30
    seminary, at Berkeley (1967), 28, 144-45
    spiritual direction, 52-57, 145
    valley fever, 20-21
Karelius, Erik (son)
    detached retina, 27-28
    disability, 3-4, 25
    at El Sanctuario de Chimayo, 23-27, 99-100
    encephalitis, 54
    the moon and, 104, 146-47
Karelius, Janice (wife)
    on addictions, 55
    on drug-induced experiences, 122-23
    Holy Sand experience, 23-27
    at Monument Valley, 3
    on moon, effects on people, 104
    as nurse-practionioner, 29
    pinyon seed gathering, 13
Karelius, Katie (daughter), 29
Karelius, Lyle (father), 9-11, 29
Karelius, Michael (brother), 138
King Tutankhamen's tomb, 20

Kinsolving, Arthur B., 12
kivas, as sacred ground, 113-18
Kushner, Harold, 29

Lamy (archbishop), 97
The Land of Poco Tiempo (Lummis), 95
Lane, Belden, 135-36
Lash of the Penitentes (film), 95
Lasiloo-Jim, Verla, 34-35
Leary, Timothy, 121, 122, 123
Lewis, C. S., 87
Lewis, George, 82, 83
Llano del Rio, 120
Lopez Pulido, Alberto, 96, 98
LSD, 121, 123-24
Luhan, Mable Dodge, 115
Lummis, Charles, 95-96
lunar eclipse
    Diné culture, 101-3
    Euro-American culture, 103-4

manna, bread of heaven, 14-15
Martin, James, 22
Marxism and monasticism, 50
Maslow, Abraham, 68
McEvilley, Thomas, 134
McManis, Kent, 33-34, 35-36
medical treatment, 105-7, 109-11
Menorah in the Night Sky (Shore), 136-37
mental illness, spirituality vs., 65-70
Merton, Thomas, 38, 40, 45-50, 119, 135
Merton: a Film Biography (film), 47
Mesa Verde National Park, Colorado, 116
mescaline, 121
Messiah Episcopal Church, Santa Ana, California, 4, 11-12
The Milagro Beanfield Wars (film), 94
Milky Way, 140
mining, in California, 83-84, 98
Ministry to the Sick ritual, 28
monasteries
    ascetical practices, 96
    Benedict of Nursia, 43-44
    Christ in the Desert at Abiquiu, New Mexico., 46, 48-51, 135-36

Index

monasteries (continued)
    Desert Fathers and Mothers, 45–46
Monastery of Christ in the Desert, New Mexico, 46
Monument Valley, Utah, 74, 76, 77–78
moon
    eclipse, Diné culture, 101–3
    eclipse, Euro-American culture, 103–4
    effects on people, 104
    Erik Karelius and, 104, 146–47
Mooney, James, 19
Moreland, Gordon, 29, 52–53, 56–57
Morrison, Jim, 121
Mose, Don, 74–76, 79–80
Mt. Calvary Episcopal Monastery, 50
mysticism, 67–70
myth, 143

Nakashima, George, 48
Napier, Johnathan, 36
narrative, identity and, 118
NASA, and the Navajo Nation, 138–140
Natalie (Hopi child), 63–64
nature, interdependency of, 131
Navajo Moon: Educational Activities Bringing Together NASA Science and Navajo Cultural Knowledge, 138
Navajo Nation, 19–20, 74–81, 105–12, 137–38
Nelson, Steffie, 121
Nez, Harry, 74, 79, 102, 147
night sky, 134–141
Noah Project, 5
noetic, defined, 67, 70
The North American Geographer (Smith), 97–98
Nouwen, Henri, 126
Nuglish, Georg and Ulla, 41–42

objective reality, 69
Olancha Creek, 71–72
Order of Deacons, 98
Orientalism (Said), 77
Osmond, Humphrey, 121

Otto, Rudolph, 70
The Oyster Review (online journal), 127

Pachomius, 44–45
Paiute People, 13, 19, 140
Pambo, Abbot, 45–46
Pascal, Blaise, 141
passive experience, defined, 67
Paul (apostle, saint), 37–38
Paulsell, William O., 52
Paya, Lemuel, 9
Peabody, Henry G., 12
"peak-experience," 68
Penitentes of Acoma, 93
Penitentes of New Mexico, 94–100
peyote, 121
pinyon seeds, 13–15
Place of Holy Sand, 23–27
poor and vulnerable populations, 98
"porous self," 37
Poverty Hills, California, 82–84
prayers and praying
    Examen of Conscience, 56–57
    fetishes and, 35, 39
    in gratitude, 73
    for healing, 8, 26–28, 30, 80
    to the Holy, 7
    Hopi prayer rituals, 61, 63
    in monasteries, 44–50
Pre-Critical Stage, 143–44
Prendiville, Paul, 87
Prezelski, Carmen, Villa, 18
"Psychiatric Drugs and Healing" (Johnston), 110
psychics, 124
psychosis, 69–71, 73
Pueblo Indians, 46
Pulido, Alberto Lopez, 96, 98

Qu'ran, 14–15

Rainbow Bridge to Monument Valley (Harvey), 77
Ram Dass (Alpert, Richard), 123
Rao (doctor), 27
reading the signs, 126–133
reason, world of, 90, 143

Index

Religious Aspects of Peak-Experiences (Maslow), 68
Remington, Bill, 3
restless souls, 84–85
Revelation, 91
Ricoeur, Paul, 118, 142, 143–44
Rolheiser, Ron, 6, 56, 65, 73, 85, 86, 145–46
Roman Catholic Church, 5, 15, 66, 96–97
Romanus (monk), 43
Ronald Lanner, 14

sacred images, 38
sacred knowledge, 108
sacred masks, 59–64
sacred objects, sale of, 59
sacred place, as defined by Navajo culture, 79–80, 128
sacred texts, 143
The Sacred World of the Penitentes (Lopez Pulido), 96, 98
Saddleback Community College, Mission Viejo, California, 6
Sagan, Carl, 138
sage, herbal medicine, 109–10
Said, Edward, 77
St. Joseph Ballet, 5
St. Joseph Workshop (Taller San Jose), 5
St. Timothy Roman Catholic Church, Laguna Niguel, California, 15
Salcinez, Raquel, 4
Salpointe (archbishop), 97
Savage, Charles, 123
Savage, Emmy, 123–24
Schucman, Helen, 68
scientific connection with the world, 90, 107, 143
The Searchers (film), 76
searching, dissatisfaction and, 84–85
A Second Childhood (Chesterton), 146
"second naiveté," 143, 146
A Secular Age (Taylor), 36
Seder, Passover Meal, 15
seeing the Divine within, 119–125
seminary, Berkeley (1967), 28

The Seven Storey Mountain (Merton), 46–47
She Wore a Yellow Ribbon (film), 76
Sheldrake, Phillip, 113, 117–18
Shore, Jacques J. M., 136
Sinagua Indians of Arizona, 18
Sinclair, Paul, 20
sipapu, 116, 118
Siwulogi (dust devils), 18
Six, Beverly G., 126
skinwalkers, 109, 130
sky, at night, 134–141
Smith, Christopher, 4
Smith, Jeffrey S., 97
soldiers, Navajo, 109
"Songs of Life Returning" (Paiute song), 19
Sperber, James, 20–21
"The Spirit Catches You and You Fall Down" (Fadiman), 110
spiritual direction, 52–57, 145
spiritual exercises
    in the desert, 92
Saint Ignatius, 54–56, 145
    using drugs, 122–23
The Spiritual Life of Children (Coles), 63
spirituality
    life-giving or destructive, 65
    mental illness vs., 65–70
    term usage, 6–7
Stagecoach (film), 76, 101
stars, purpose of, 103
Stations of the Cross, 99
stone fetishes, 33–35
Stylites, Simon, 96
Sunset Crater Volcano National Monument, 89
Swanson, John, 39

Talking God (Hillerman), 60
Taller San Jose (St. Joseph's Workshop), 5
Taylor, Carl N., 98
Taylor, Charles, 6–7, 36–37
Teresa of Avila (saint), 69
Thomas, Roger, 32
Thoreau, Henry David, 73

Index

Thoughts in Solitude (Merton), 47
transient, defined, 67
transparency and honesty, 56
Trappist Community of Gethsemane, Kentucky, 46–47, 50
treasure, searching for, 82–86
trees, mediation on, 90–91

Underhill, Evelyn, 67
Upfield, Arthur W., 129
Urell , John, 30

valley fever (coccidioidomycosis), 20–21
Varieties of Religious Experience (James), 67
Vazquez, David, 5

Walking in the Way of Jesus in his Passion of the Cross, 94–95, 97, 99
Wallace, Bill, 65

Walpi Mesa, 113–15
Wapnick, Kenneth, 68
Wasson, R. Gordon, 123
water project, for Havasupai people, 9–11
Watson, Editha, 79–80
Wayne, John, 76, 101
Weber, Max, 68
Weigle, Marta, 97
whirlwind, biblical passages on, 19
Wild Medicinal Herbs of the United States (Henkel), 111
The Wisdom of the Desert (Merton), 47–48
witches, 109, 130
world, connections with, 90–91

X-Files (television show), 126–27

Zoeller, Jeffrey, 49
Zuni Pueblo, 32–39

www.ingramcontent.com/pod-product-compliance
Lightning Source LLC
Chambersburg PA
CBHW051931160426
43198CB00012B/2108